How to Paint Flowers In Water Colors
Step by Step Lessons

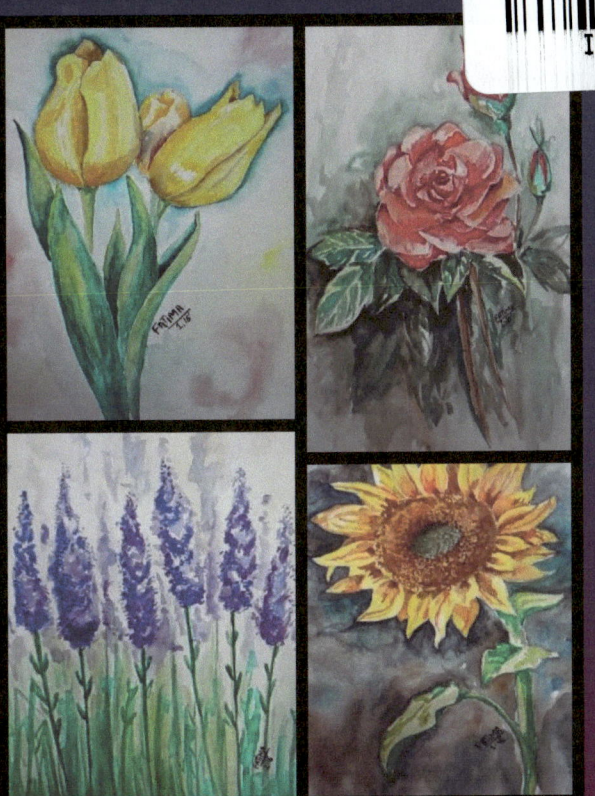

Fatima Usman

Learn to Draw Series

Mendon Cottage Books

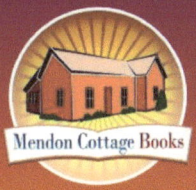

JD-Biz Publishing

Our books are available at

1. Amazon.com
2. Barnes and Noble
3. Itunes
4. Kobo
5. Smashwords
6. Google Play Books

Download Free Books!

http://MendonCottageBooks.com

Table of Contents

Introduction

It is not difficult! I guess this line will open the doors of hope for you. And I'm not just bragging. It sure is one of the most difficult mediums to paint with and that was exactly the challenge I accepted when I started my Arts education. I thought, how difficult can it really be? I have realized over the time that everything in this world is difficult only until you learn it. If you try, you do get a grasp of it sooner or later. One very important thing is that you find someone who can teach you, and can teach you well.

Here I hope I will be able to transfer as much knowledge as I can in a possibly detailed manner. If you were in a class, I would be open to questions. But that is not the case in our situation, so I want to make sure that by the time you finish this book, you won't have any questions left. I am keeping the struggles in my mind, that I made just to learn this technique and how I wished I could get one person or a single book that could be my fairy god mother and teach me everything I needed to know in a wave of a wand. That didn't happen, of course. But I did learn and now that I know, I want to transfer my knowledge to you.

Why is water color one of the difficult materials? Everybody has their own reasons; the only reason that I am going to tell you is that they are a bit hard to control. Don't worry! Don't be taken aback. I'm here to teach you. This book contains activities by which you will learn to control your color, brush strokes, and many other things.

I assure you that you have made the best choice. You will not only learn to paint flowers and many other things that your heart desires because you will learn to use your brush and get familiar with different materials and techniques.

I would like to wish you best of luck and hope that your, and my hard work will pay in the form of you being as good as me or even better.

About Watercolors

Short History

Water colors are also called Aquarelle which is a French word. Aquarelle means water. In these paints, the colors are made of pigments mixed in water based liquid. Water color painting bloomed in England, somewhere in the eighteenth century. Basically water colors history goes as far back as cave men. The cave men were actually the first people who used colors that were water based to paint their ritual paintings in caves. They used their hands and fingers to paint different animals on cave walls. The ancient Egyptians also used water based paints to tell their stories. They painted stories of power, drought, and blessings on their walls. The Egyptians also painted on paper that was made of papyrus with water based colors. The Chinese and Japanese also used water colors for their works. These artists worked on fabric and used silk as their work surface to paint literature and calligraphy. Chinese calligraphy is renowned throughout the world and many Chinese artists still use water based inks. After that, from China the tradition was taken to western world. The Indians and Persians used water based paints in their works of decoration, and the Muslims used them to show their religious history.

Paper, of course, played its role in flourishing of our beloved water colors. We can give the credit to Chinese. Chinese were very good at creating paper. They had handmade papers of the best quality. In the eighth century, the Arabs came to know their ways of making papers. Europeans imported paper for a long time until they managed to open their own mill in Italy. In early ages paper was considered a great luxury as it was very expensive. This was one of the major reasons why the water color paintings did not flourish for a long time. When paper became available to people the great artists like Leonardo de Vinci started using it for their drawings. Albrecht Durer, a German artist, is known to be the first master of water colors. Among his many paintings, *The Owl* is worth seeing and worth studying. The depth of the eyes and the softness of the bird are very evident.

Water color is a type of medium that is very unpredictable. A water colorist, in most of the cases and techniques has to be fast. This comes with time and experience. The more you paint, the more you learn. Trial and error does count. In water color all the colors are water based. Be it water color tubes or cakes. It depends on individual artist what he/she is comfortable with; otherwise, the pan and the tube colors work the same. There isn't much difference as far as you are using good quality brands. For a beginner it is better to use affordable beginner's paints. Usually it is mentioned on the box as 'Beginners Quality'.

Types of Water Colors

There are mainly two types of water colors that you can find in the market. One is Opaque water colors and the other is Transparent water colors. As you would have guessed by their names, the Opaque water colors are 'opaque'. That means they would not give you a transparent effect. The opaque colors give a rather solid effect than watery. These colors are usually not used by professional artists. The reason might be that it kills the whole idea of 'Water' in it. Fair enough I guess!

The professionals usually prefer to use the second type of water colors, the 'transparent water colors'. Transparent water colors, as the name suggests, are 'transparent'. You can see the paper through the colors. These types of colors are not only professional, they have beautiful effects. Many textures can be achieved by using transparent water colors. Here I would like to add that these transparent water colors are also used as solid colors by many artists to paint intricate designs. For example, Arabesque is an ornamental art that is very intricate and is usually painted on paper using transparent water colors with solidity.

Water color is done on paper usually. There are many types of papers that I will further explain in coming chapters. The papers not only differ in textures, they also differ in weight. Water colors are used on other surfaces also. These include wood, bark paper, leather, fabric, and even canvas. Every surface has its own pros and cons. On some surfaces, water colors become more difficult to use, for e.g., wood is too absorbent. There cannot be a comparison between surfaces and their difficulty level or, which surface gives you the best results. On canvas we cannot achieve as many textures as we can on paper. On paper also, the techniques differ, and with technique differs the rate of absorbency. Nothing is certain in water colors.

Every artist has their own expertise. All have different views about different surfaces. Whatever you get good at becomes easy for you. Above all, whatever you enjoy will not only be easy for you, but you will also learn and excel in that field. All I can say is, water color are learnt with passion and done with passion.

Different Techniques of Watercolor painting

Every medium has a lot of techniques of painting. In water colors there are mainly two techniques. One is layering the other is direct painting. In direct water color painting you apply the paint with strength of light medium dark directly for the first time.

In the layering technique paint is applied in layers. First we apply the lightest tone and then work on it as we go further. In this book I am using layering technique because it is easily understood.

Flowers in Water Colors

When painting, we will not only paint the flowers alone. The stems and leaves come with it. Here I will also show you how to paint the stems and leaves. There is no different technique in painting them. The only thing is that the stems are pretty thin in contrast to the flowers; therefore, they are often ignored and painted in one shade by many beginners. I do realize that it is okay for a beginner to paint a few surfaces flat (flat is a term used to describe the area that is painted in one tone). I am pointing this out to you in advance, so you can keep in mind while painting that even the thinnest parts like a stem could also be given shades, I would at least try it. However, I have included an exercise of shading thin areas in this book.

There are many types of flowers, for example, there are buds, fully bloomed flowers, and half bloomed flowers. Some flowers stand tall on stems facing the sky, while others peep on sides. There are petals that stretch alone in front of the background and petals that overlap. Some flowers hang and some grow in clusters. I know, you already know all this but I am bringing it up to make you understand that each type of flower has a different light source. Taking sun as our light source here; the uplifted flowers get light from top while the side facing flower's have it on their upper sides. On the flowers that face downwards, the light hits their bottom. The clustered flowers have altogether a different type of effect of light. In clusters like Hydrangeas, there are two types of shadings. One within the cluster and the other affects the overall shape of the bunch. The change of light source can change the shading too but the basic technique of shading remains the same. The key to good shading is trying to capture the lights and darks.

Comparison with Other Mediums

Every medium has its own specialty. Water colors differ from other mediums, as they give a very transparent effect. They stand out due to transparency and technique.

Oil Paints

Oil paints are used with oil and they are very creamy. Oil paints are ideal for very large paintings. They take a very long time to dry, whereas water color dries very quickly. This is a plus point and a negative one too. You don't have to wait too long to work further. But you have to be very quick while painting. This is the reason why water colors are not used for huge paintings.

Acrylic Paints

Acrylic paints are water based. They can also be used like water colors but you cannot achieve the transparent effects of water colors in it. Acrylics are a bit shinier than oil paints but unlike oil paints, they dry very quickly.

Others

There are other mediums too, like pencil sketching, color pencils, pastels etc. They have an entirely different look and, as you may know they are applied directly, not painted.

Materials used for water color painting

Material for drawing

Pencil, sharpener, and eraser, for obvious reasons.

Tracing Paper

This is used to transfer image from picture to paper.

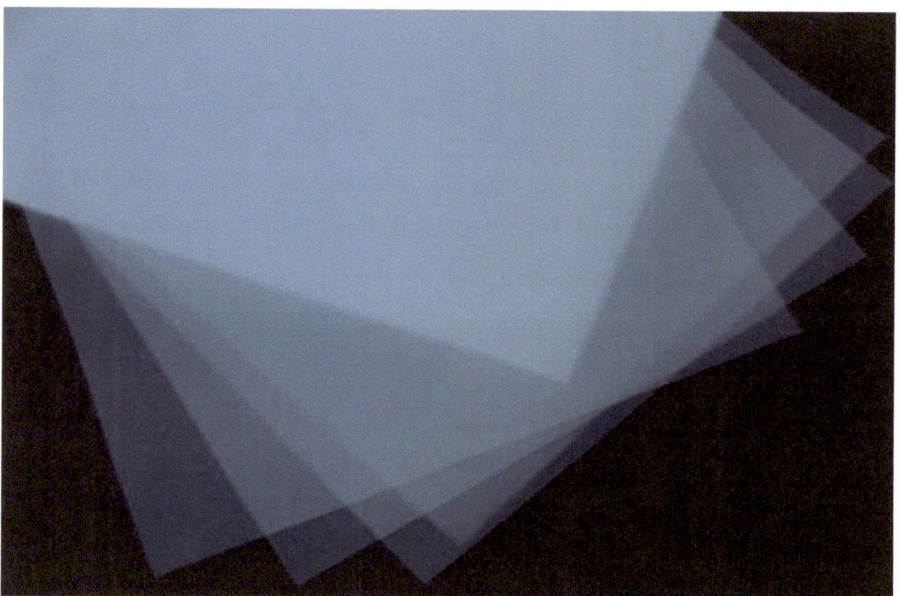

Water colors

Of course you've got to have water colors in some form. You can use color pans or tubes. It won't matter a lot as far as you are comfortable using the kind.

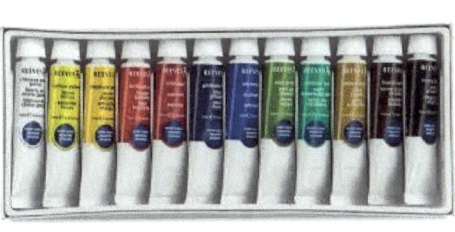 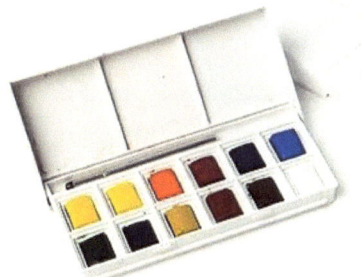

Paper

You will need a surface to work on. Water colors are usually done on paper, so you will need one too. There are different types of papers. All papers have different weights. You can find papers in 90lb, 140lb, and also 300lb. If you are a beginner you can simply buy a 90lb paper pad.

Pallet

These are available in many shapes and sizes. Make sure you buy one with a lot of compartments. This will help you in mixing colors.

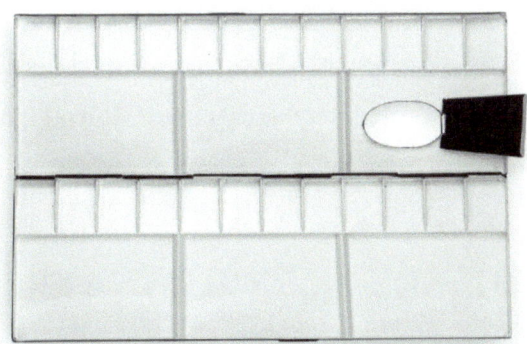

Brushes

Brushes have many types. For water colors round brushes are ideal. Many artists use different brushes like fan brush, flat brush, or angled brushes for some effects. For a beginner, round brushes of few sizes will be enough.

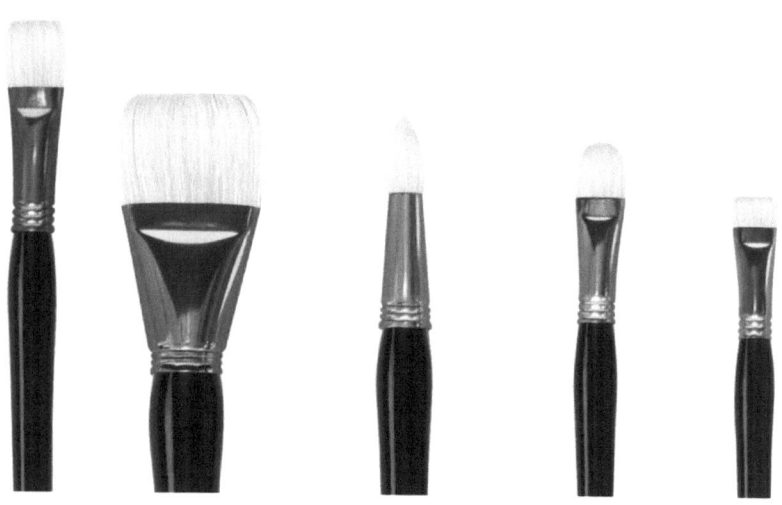

Masking fluid

It is a fluid used to help you leave white areas in the painting. It does have other purposes like you can secure a layer and paint it afterwards. Not a necessity though. Many professional artists use it. But a lot of water color artists are experienced enough to leave white spaces without help of masking fluid.

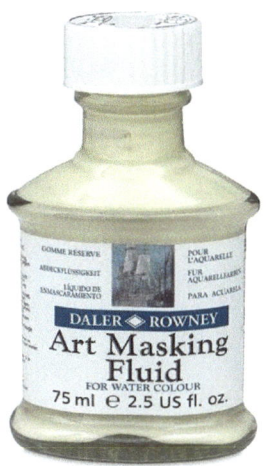

Containers

You will need two containers filled with water. One is to wash the paint off the brush and the other one is to rewash the brush. There is no specific type of containers. Make sure they are not too light weighted because sometimes due to less weight, the containers fall and you can ruin your entire workplace or even your painting. Scary, isn't it? Just be careful! Use an old glass or mug and you will do fine.

Tissue Paper

You will need some tissue papers to wipe your brushes. It helps you to take access water off the paint brush.

Board

You will need a board if you are using a sheet. If it is 300lb paper, it will do without a board. For any other paper less than weight of 300lb, you have to spread it on a board with masking tape.

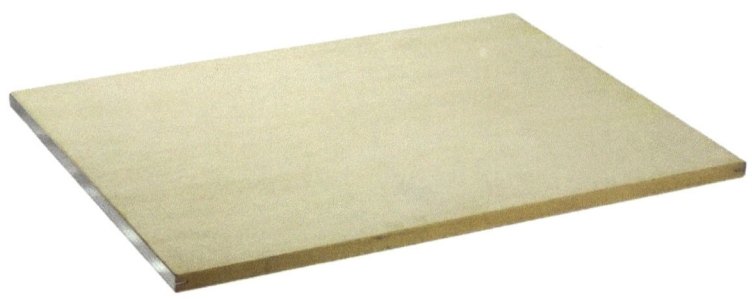

Masking Tape

Used to secure all four sides of the sheet and stick it to the board. It comes in three sizes. Small paper just requires the thin size.

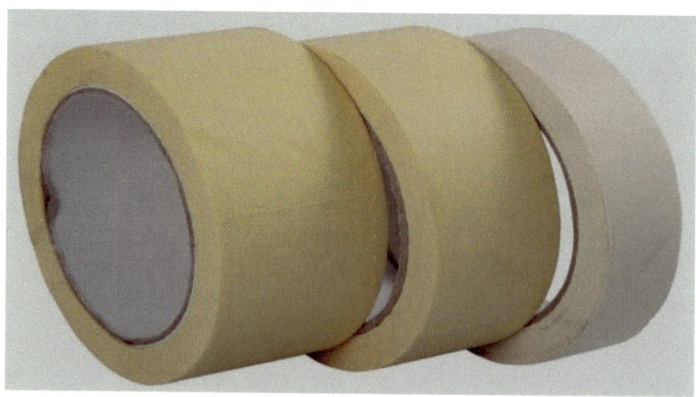

Hair Dryer

You will need it to dry your paint. It also helps in taking off masking tape without damaging the sheet.

Materials needed in this book for painting

What am I using in this book for painting? All of the above accept the masking fluid. You can do without a hair dryer too. Only that, you will have to wait for some layers to dry. Following are a few details about what you will exactly need to paint your flowers. You will need a pencil, eraser, sharpener, tracing paper, and a sheet, as I have told you earlier; you can simply buy a water color pad and paint on that. It is advisable to take the paper out of your pad and stick it to the board. If you are looking for a sheet, use 90lb for start. If you can't find a pad with paper weight mentioned on it, you can buy the one that says it is good for water colors. A tissue paper.

I prefer pan colors. You can use tube colors if you feel better with them. You will need a board, a masking tape, and containers for water and brushes. To finish the exercises in this book, you will need a flat 1.5 inch brush. No2, No4, and No8 size round brushes. Flat 1.5inch brush is used to wet the larger surface areas like background. No8 brush is used to paint the background. Other brushes will help you paint the flowers.

Primary and Secondary Colors

Primary colors are the colors that cannot be made by mixing any other colors. They are red, blue, and yellow. Secondary colors are the ones that we attain by mixing primary colors.

Red+Blue=Purple

Blue+Yellow=Green

Yellow+Red=Orange

So the secondary colors are Purple, Green, and Orange.

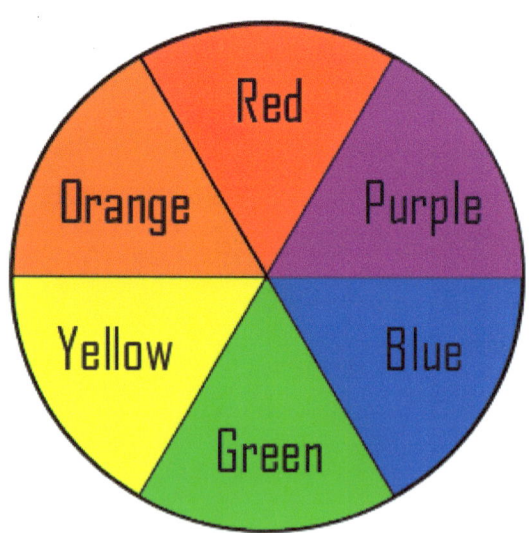

Color Wheel and its significance

Color wheel contains all six colors, red, blue, and yellow; then how they mix up to make purple, green, and orange, the secondary colors. A color wheel is important because it makes you understand better how colors are mixed. There are also detailed color wheels which explain other different shades of colors too. Another importance of a color wheel is that you can choose color schemes from it. It's like having readymade schemes for your paintings or designs.

Practice Activities

Three tones

Exercise#1

This is a very simple exercise. This exercise will teach you the difference between three tones that we are going to use in our paintings. It is not necessary that only three tones are used in a painting but mostly these three fit into each painting. Here it is important to note that in water colors, many tones are made automatically with the quantity of water on the paper. Also, the quantity of water on the paper matters a lot in making a tone lighter or darker. Usually you mix the paint with water and dilute it to a point where you think it will give you the results needed. In the end, the dilution of paint and the fact that how wet the surface is, both determine the tonal quality.

For this exercise, draw three circles. Take a No 3 round brush and make it wet. A slight dip in water will be sufficient. Take excess water off the brush. Make the surface area of circle wet as if you were doing it with color. Dilute blue color with water and make sure that you have diluted well. Paint the circle and leave it alone. You can see the result of one layer of paint in the first circle marked as 'light' this is the lightest tone achieved by giving a very light wash of color.

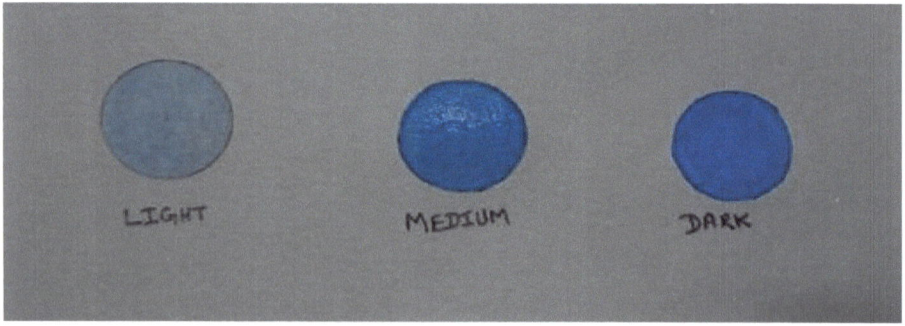

For the second circle, do the same as you did for the first one. After the first coat, apply another coat, and another if necessary. Same goes for the third circle. Repeat the steps and add a bit more color. Try diluting it with less water to get darkest tone better. When doing this activity, be careful to finish your work before the surface area of circle gets dry. Try to do this in several colors. You will have a better hold of your medium when you start with flowers.

Shading

Exercise#2

In this exercise I will explain you about shading. In our previous exercise (Ex#1) we have practiced three tones, each in a different circle. Here I will show you how to use these three tones in one place. Again we will use a circle to practice because it saves you from looking out for the corners. A circle is also easy to render as compared to a triangle or square. This is because of the freedom of movement of brush in it.

Using your compass, draw a circle. I am using Burnt sienna here, you can use any color. Just make sure it is not a light tone like lemon yellow or you will have difficulty producing darker tones. Take a No 3 round brush and make it wet. Dip the brush in water slightly then Take excess water off the brush. Make the surface area of circle wet. Take your paint on the brush and start with one side of circle. You can see that left side of image2.1 is darker. This is because I did not retake any paint. I made up my mind to paint that side darker. Just spread the paint you already have to the other side. Then take more paint and repeat the process. Start from left and spread it to other parts. You can add paint as required.

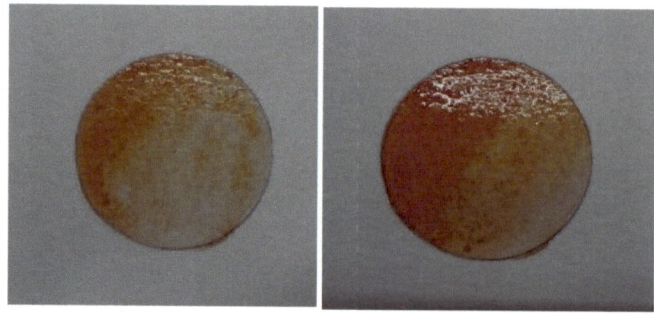

Image2.1   Image2.2

In image 2.2 you can see all the three tones. Repeat this exercise with two different colors.

Exercise#3

Using a compass, draw a circle. I am using Burnt sienna and lemon yellow, you can use any colors. Take a No 3 round brush and dip it in the water slightly then Take excess water off the brush. Make the surface area of circle wet. Take your paint on the brush and start with one side of circle. You can see that upper side of circle (image 3.1) is in Burnt sienna. In this exercise I have taken paint in handsome quantity. Take lemon yellow for the other end on the circle and start with the other side. In image 3.2 you can see how I have left a little gap between two colors. Next step is to blend. Blend both colors together with the help of a wet brush to get the final results (Image 3.3)

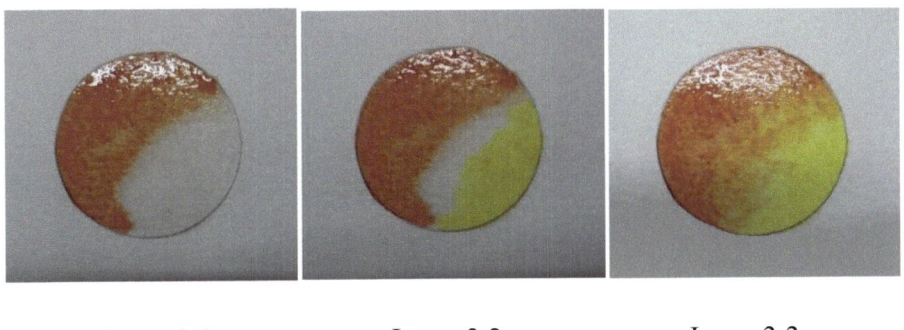

| Image3.1 | Image3.2 | Image3.3 |

Exercise#4

Using a compass, draw a circle. I am using Burnt sienna, lemon yellow, and cardamom red, you can use any colors. Take a No 3 round brush. Dip the brush in water slightly then take excess water off the brush. Make the surface area of circle wet. Take your paint on the brush, start with one side of circle and go around it (Image 4.1). You can see that upper left side of circle has more color than other sides. If you feel like going around the circle will be difficult, you can simply paint one third of it. This way it is a bit more playful. Then paint the yellow and merge it like you did in the previous exercise to get results like Image4.2. In the end, take your red paint and drop it in the area that's left. Merge!

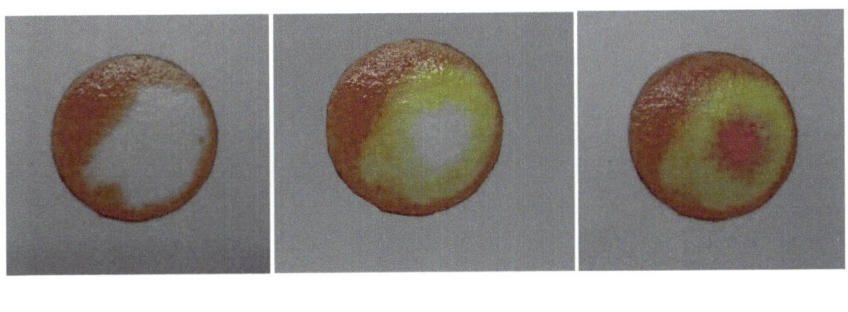

| Image 4.1 | Image 4.2 | Image 4.3 |

Exercise#5

Yes! This is what I told you about. A thin portion, as thin as a stem can also be shaded. Here draw a thin rectangle 4mm wide and 1.5" long. Make the surface area wet with the help of No 2 brush. Take a color, a color of your choice and on the upper end (image5) paint a line. The line you have painted will automatically merge in water and give you the two shades as shown in the image below. See! That's pretty easy.

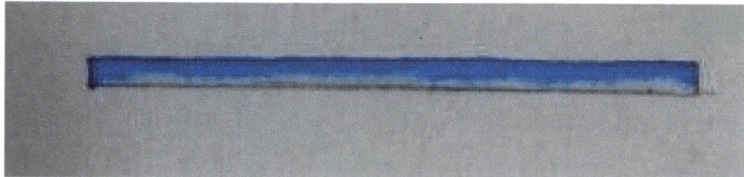

Image 5

Exercise#6

This exercise is more or less like exercise #5. You just have to draw a freehand curved line. Make it thin from one end and a bit thicker on the other end. Use your No2 brush and make the surface wet with slightly colored water. Or you can say a highly diluted paint. After you have done it. Take some paint and try to paint lines as you did in exercise #5.

Here I want you to take a close look at image 6.2. As I have painted this wave I made sure that left side had more water than the right side. So as I painted the lower line of left side, the paint spread and made a medium tone.

The right side the surface was not very wet. I painted the upper side of wave; the paint stayed and gave a darker tone. At the very right end the surface was dry so I was able to actually paint a fine line.

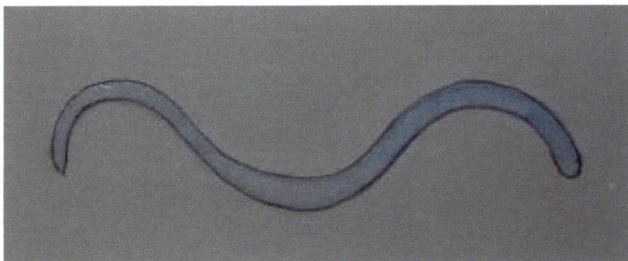

Image 6.1

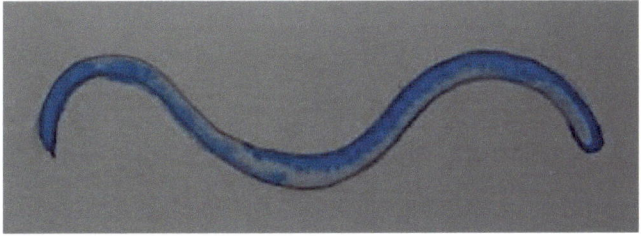

Image 6.2

Try to practice this so you can actually get hold of the basic technique of water colors. I would advise you to practice the same technique on a wider area too.

How to Draw

Free hand drawing

Free hand drawing is drawing by hand. You can simply look at the image and draw if you are good at sketching. I would appreciate if you try drawing. But if you are not too good at copying the image, it would be preferable to trace it.

Tracing

Being a beginner, I will advise you to use a picture to work from, instead of an actual still life of flowers. Doing this has a few advantages. First of all, your light source will not change, if you take a few days to complete the painting, the flowers will wither. If you have a picture of what you are painting, you don't have to worry about withering and you can take as much time as you want to complete your painting. You can trace the picture for your drawing. A perfect drawing makes it easier to paint and copy the lights and darks. If you are good at drawing then go for it. Don't trace, Draw your heart out. If you are one of those people who are eager to paint and drawing seems a long process to you, or even if you cannot draw to perfection, then trace! There is no harm in it.

Take a tracing sheet and trace the image. Then transfer it to the sheet where you want to paint.

Flower Painting Lessons

How to paint Lavenders

You will have to draw. The drawing does not have to be perfect. Just follow the lead of Image 7.1.

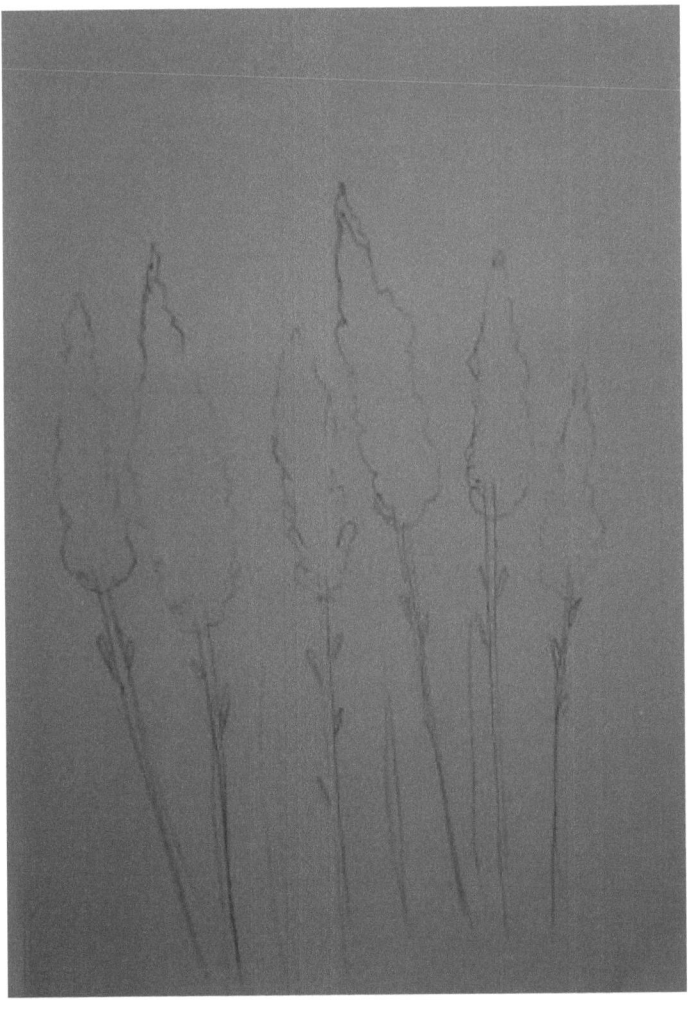

Image 7.1

Erase the lines to make them lighter. Make sure you don't erase them entirely. Moisten the background with water using a 1 inch brush. Then use some yellow ocher and shades of your favorite green for painting the background. Make sure that you make the background the lightest tone see image 7.2. We will work on the background later.

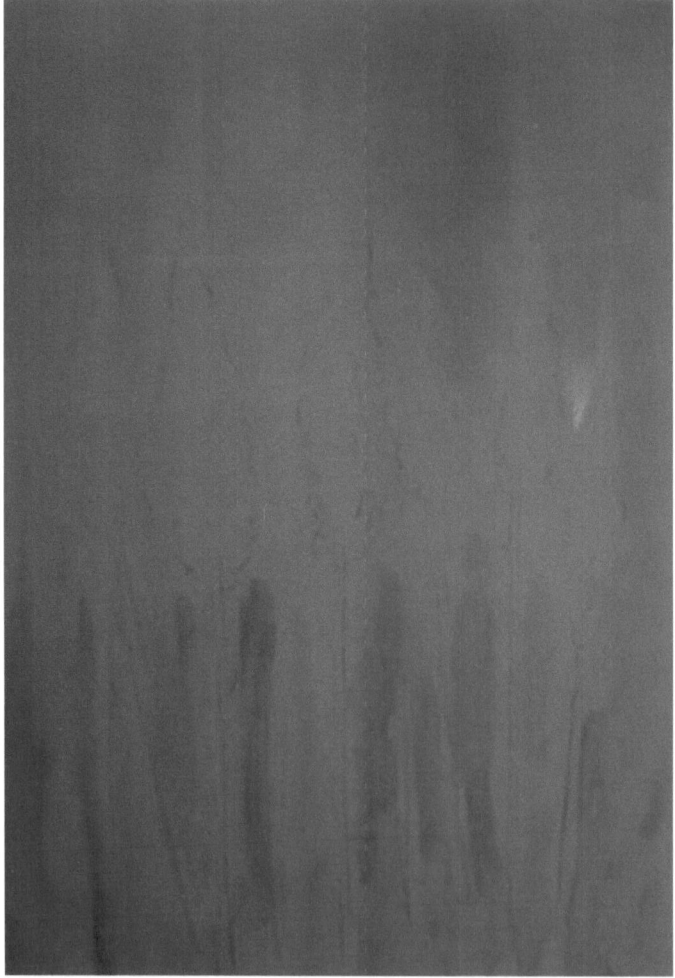

Image7.2

Use purple to mark your dark areas. We are using a light wash to mark the dark areas. This will give you an idea of how the painting will go on. In Image 7.3 you can see on one lavender steam, how this light wash will later take a darker tone. Paint steams with sap green.

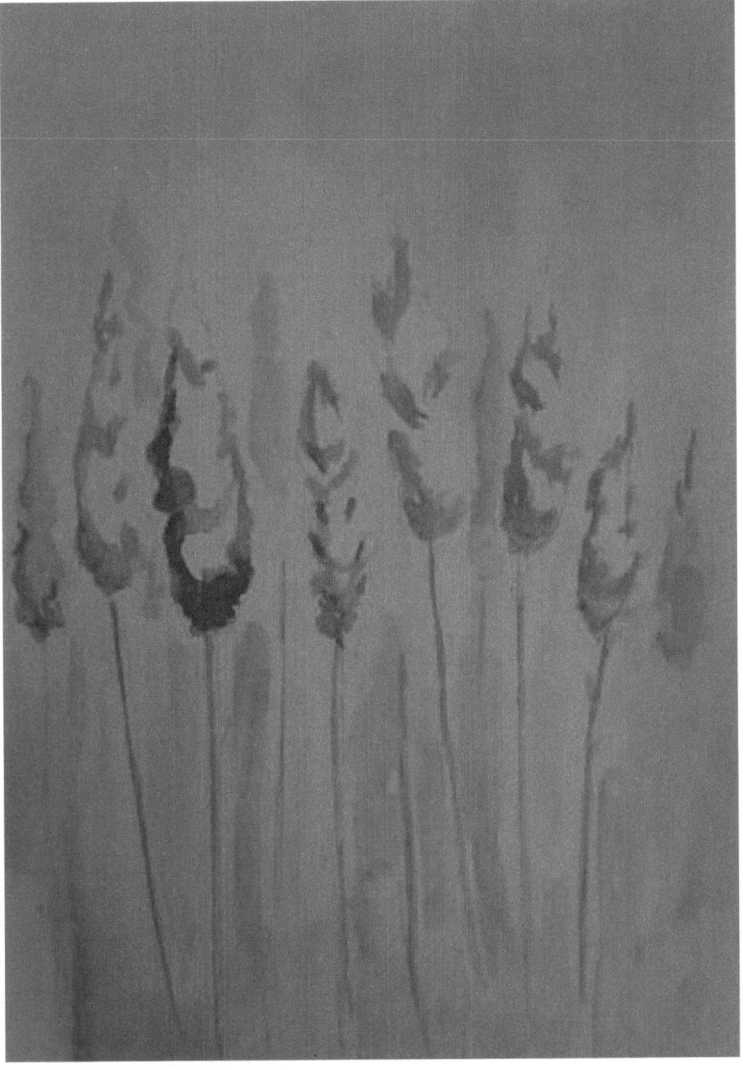

Image 7.3

Start putting the darker tones (see 7.4). You will use the same purple mixed with a little bit of blue, preferably ultramarine blue.

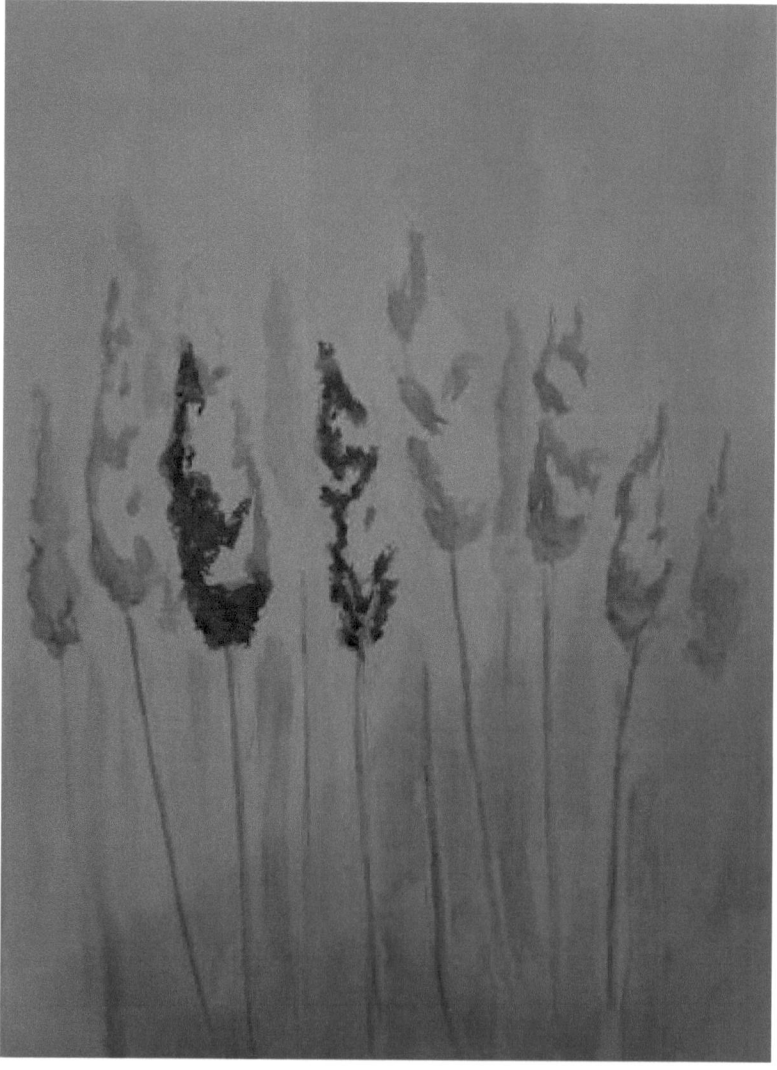

Image7.4

After painting the dark tones you have to paint the middle tones. Then give very light washes (same as you used in the first step) to make the lightest tones. Hold your brush in 90 degree angle and dab it in slight strokes to get the effect as shown in Image 7.5.

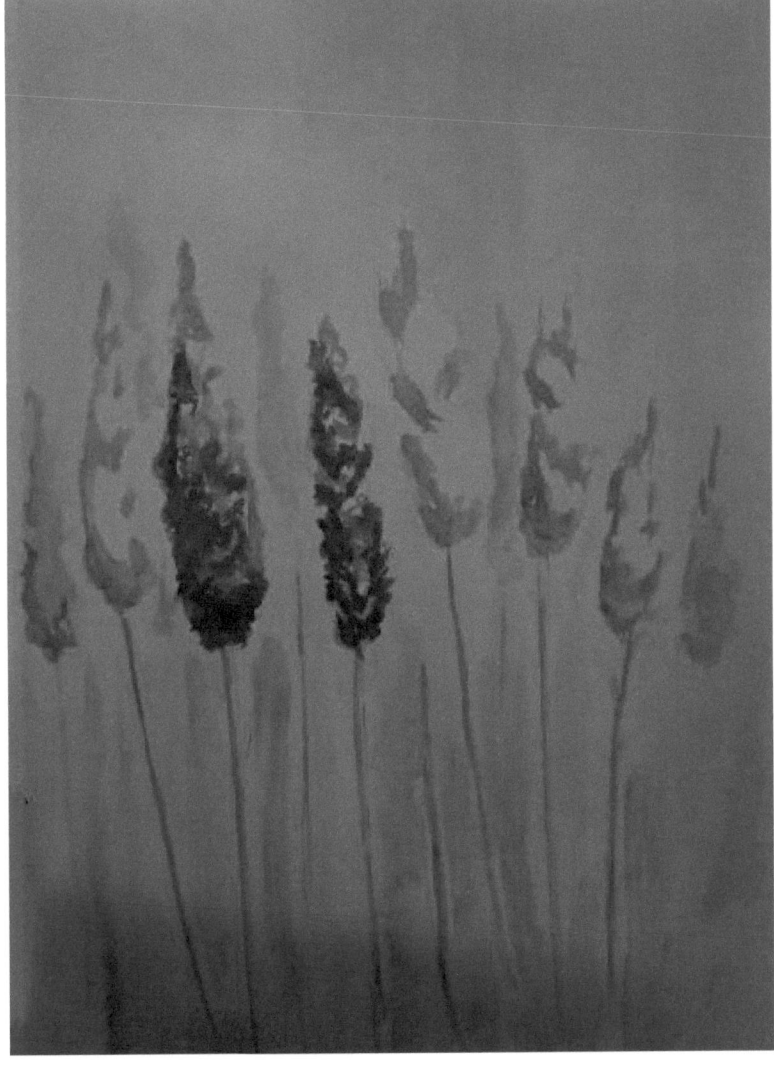

Image 7.5

Paint all the flowers in the same way.

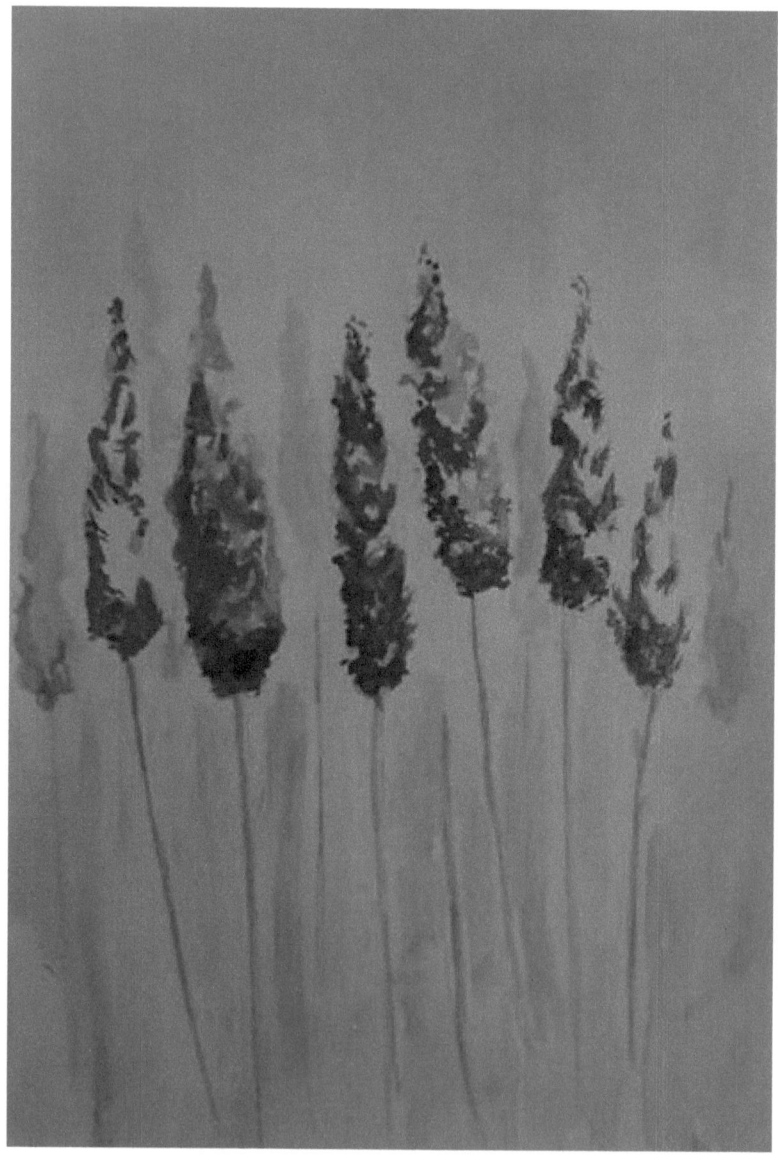

Image 7.6

After painting the main flowers, take some very diluted purple paint and make few lavender like strokes in the background (see image 7.7) also use your Hooker's green mixed with blue to make the stems prominent.

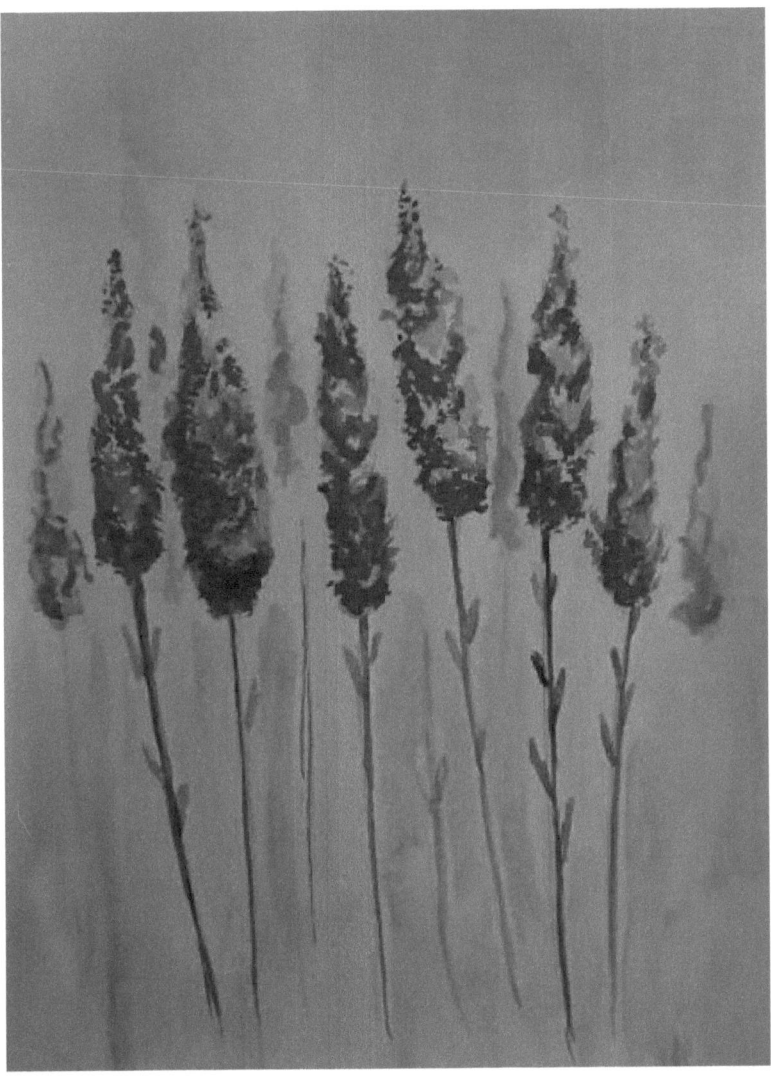

Image7.7

In the end, to add a little dramatic look, take vibrant greens and paint the base in many different shades. Try making some grass with the help of Sap green. Your painting is Complete. Sign it and show off!

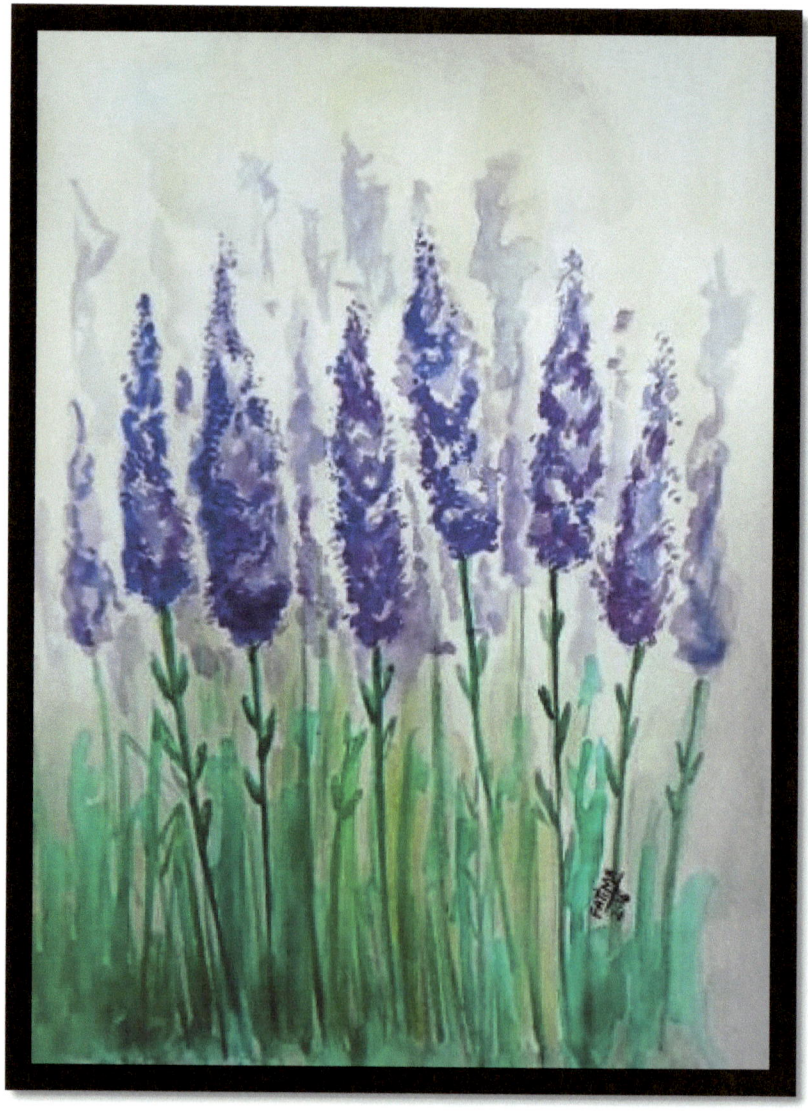

Image7.8

How to paint a rose in water colors

Roses, most probably one of the most loved flowers in the world. First of all, find a picture of a rose that you fall in love with. Trace the rose with a tracing paper and transfer it onto your sheet (See Image 8.1).

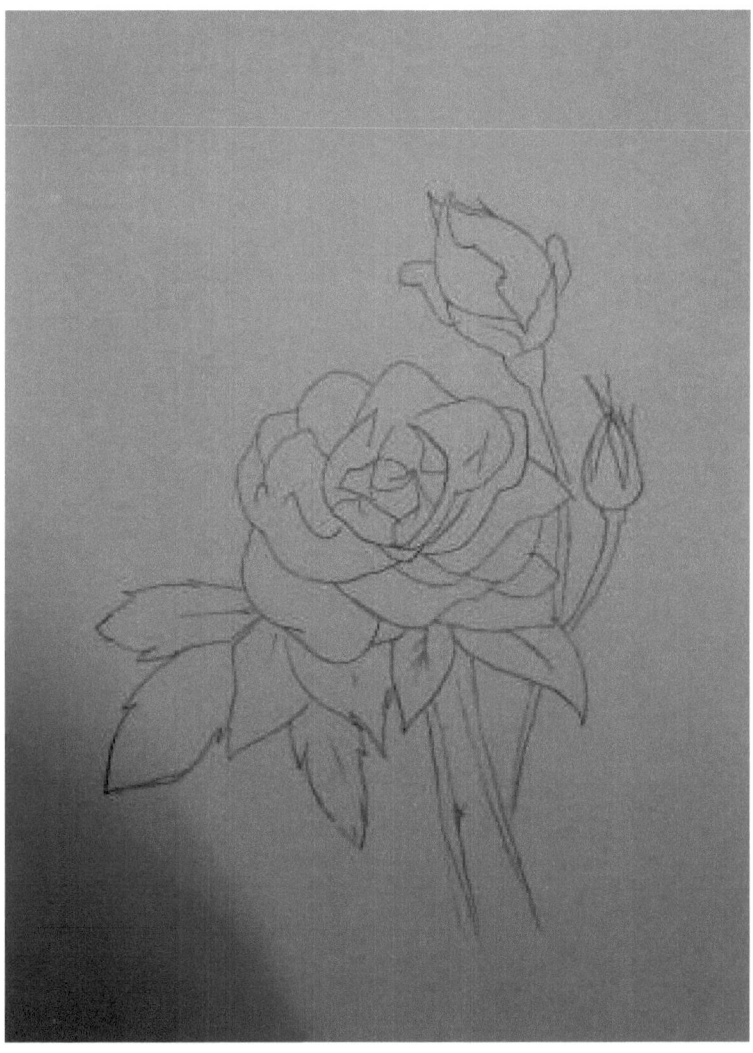

Image 8.1

Wet the background with your No8 paintbrush. Be sure that you only make the background wet and not the drawing itself. This will help you stay in control while painting background. Your paint will spread but won't go into the boundaries of the drawing. Paint the background (image 8.2). Paint it in light tones of hooker's green and burnt sienna. Try to be playful but make sure you take much diluted paint. This will help keep the colors in control.

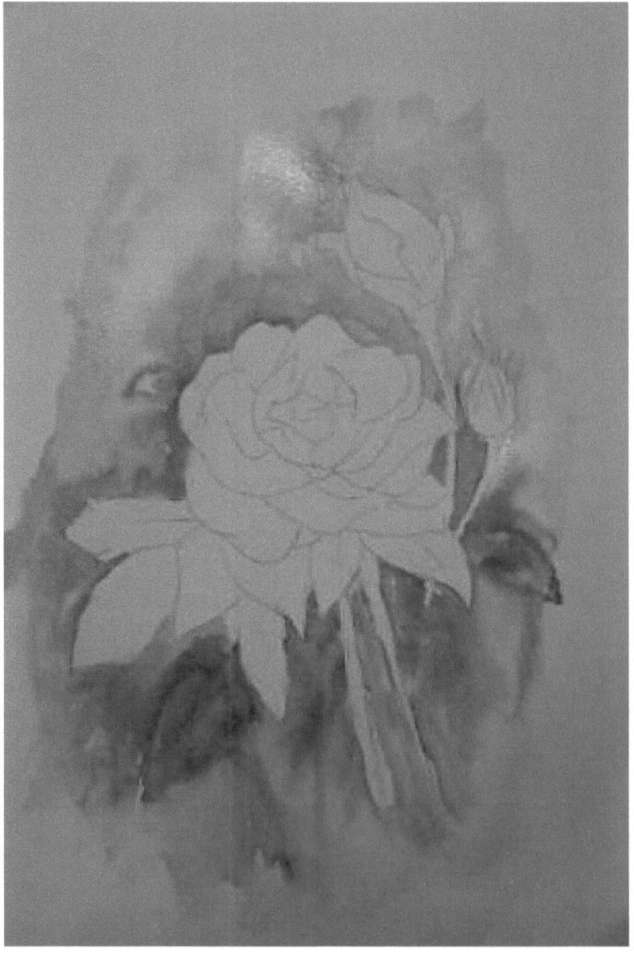

Image 8.2

It would be better if you don't let the whole surface dry entirely. Use a little darker tone to paint over the light tone. Take out some shapes. Draw some leaf like shapes. Move your brush like you were making steams. Follow the lead of image 8.3

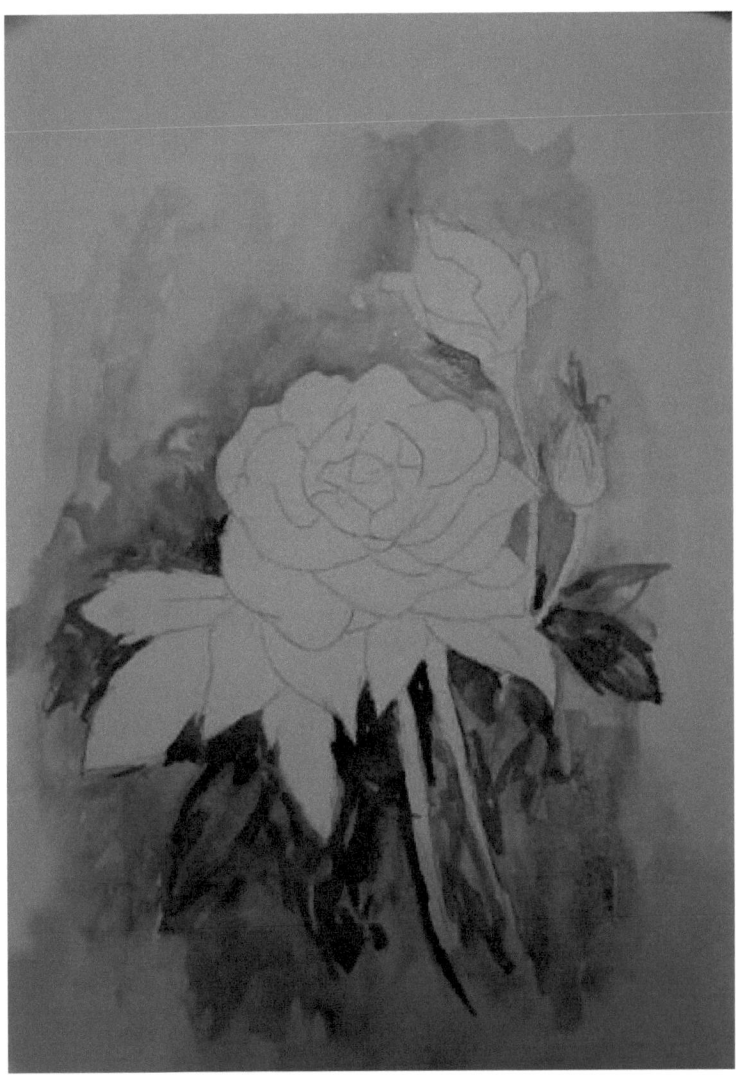

Image 8.3

The background is complete. You can always make changes in it afterwards. I will explain you how to do that in the next painting. Let's start with the flower and the buds. Take cadmium red hue and paint the whole flower in light tone. This will give you a base to work on.

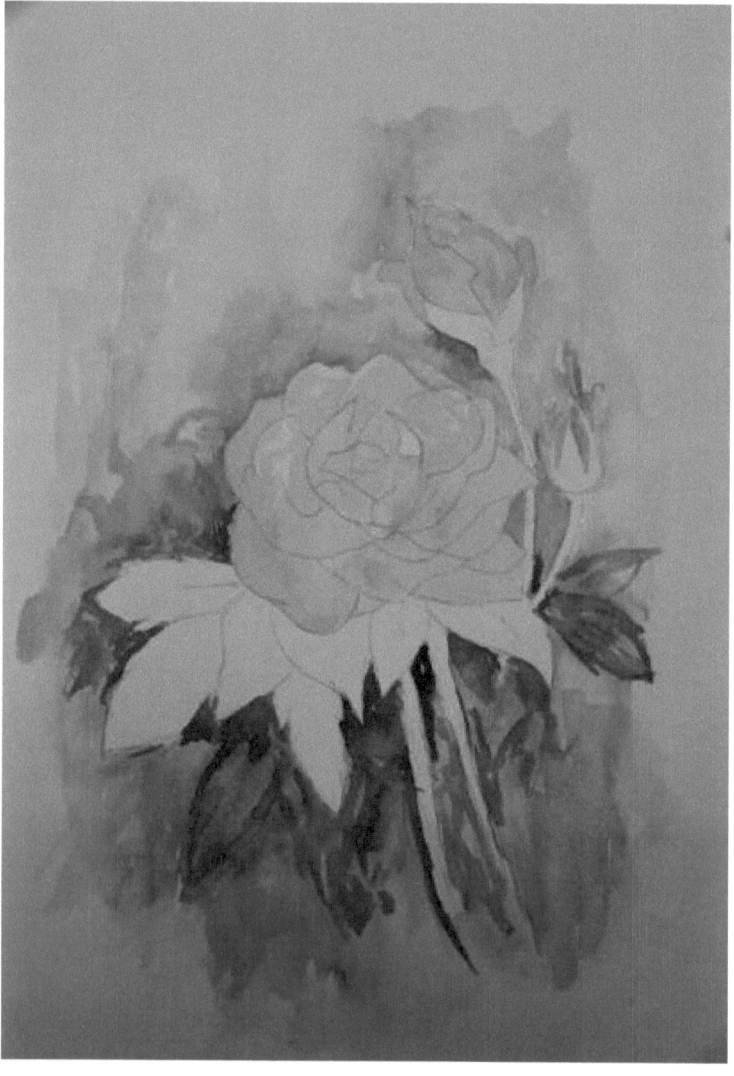

Image 8.4

Start adding darks to the petals. Start from the petals that are being overlapped. Here we will also start painting our leaves. Use your deep red for the darks. Use Hooker's green and sap green for leaves. Keep rendering the background where needed.

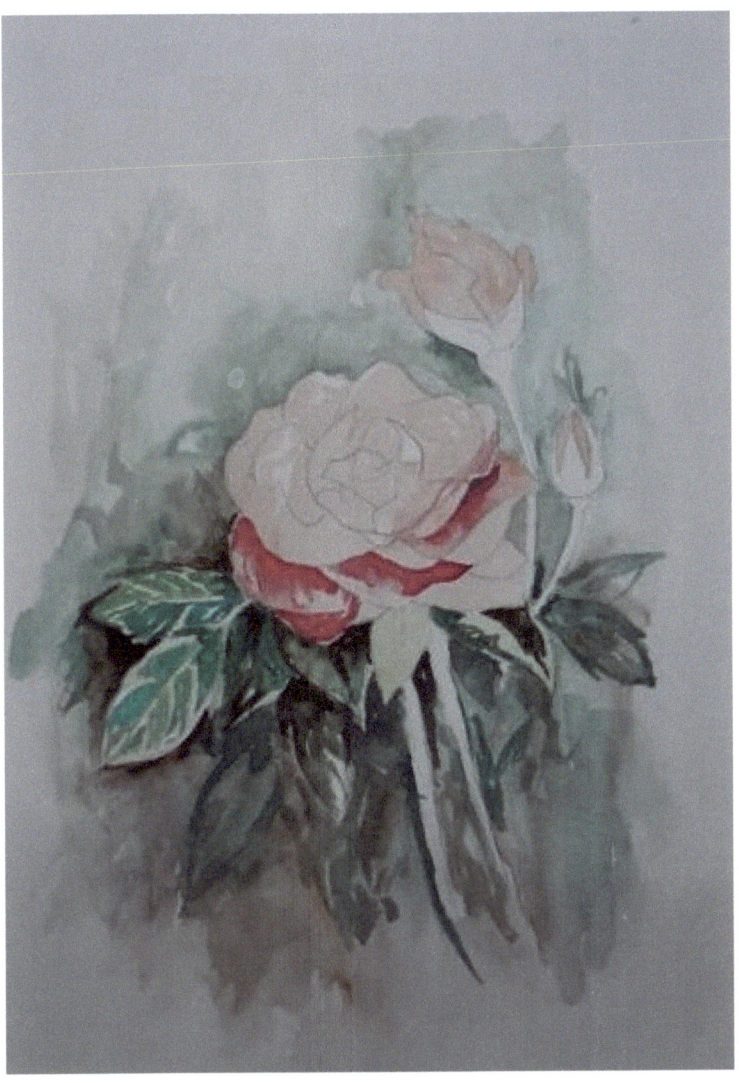

Image8.5

Here I have added all the darks. Add darks along the lines so you can make the above petal appear (image 8.6). Paint the stem with Burnt umber. Don't forget to put appropriate shading in it. If you have practiced your activities in this book, this step won't be a problem for you.

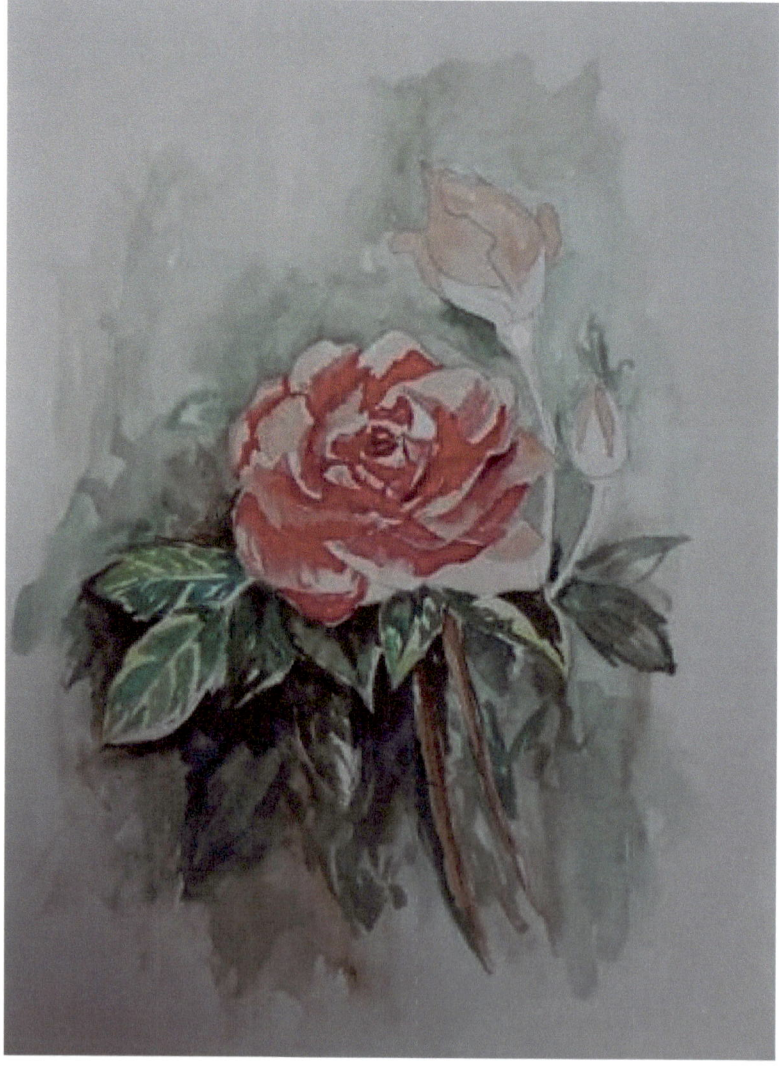

Image8.6

Complete the flower by adding middle tomes. You can add yellow to give the light tones or just leave the surface as it is (image8.7)

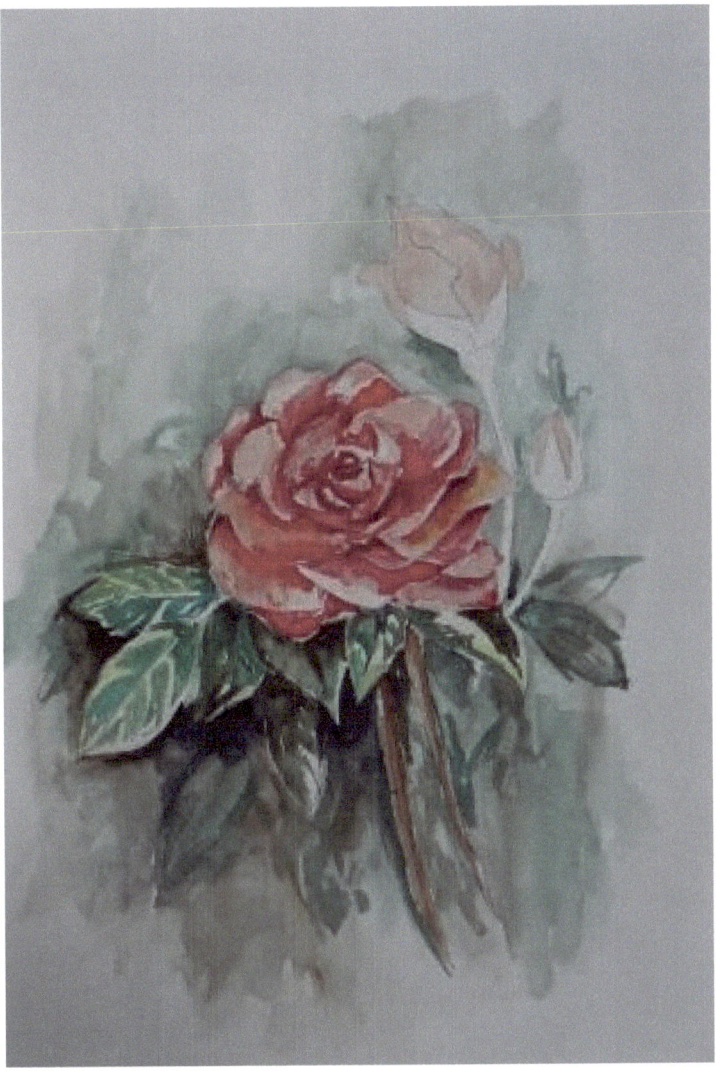

Image 8.7

Last, but not the least. Paint the buds. Paint them as you painted the flower (image7.8). Your painting is complete. Now the best part, Sign it! Give yourself a pat on back. You have done a great job.

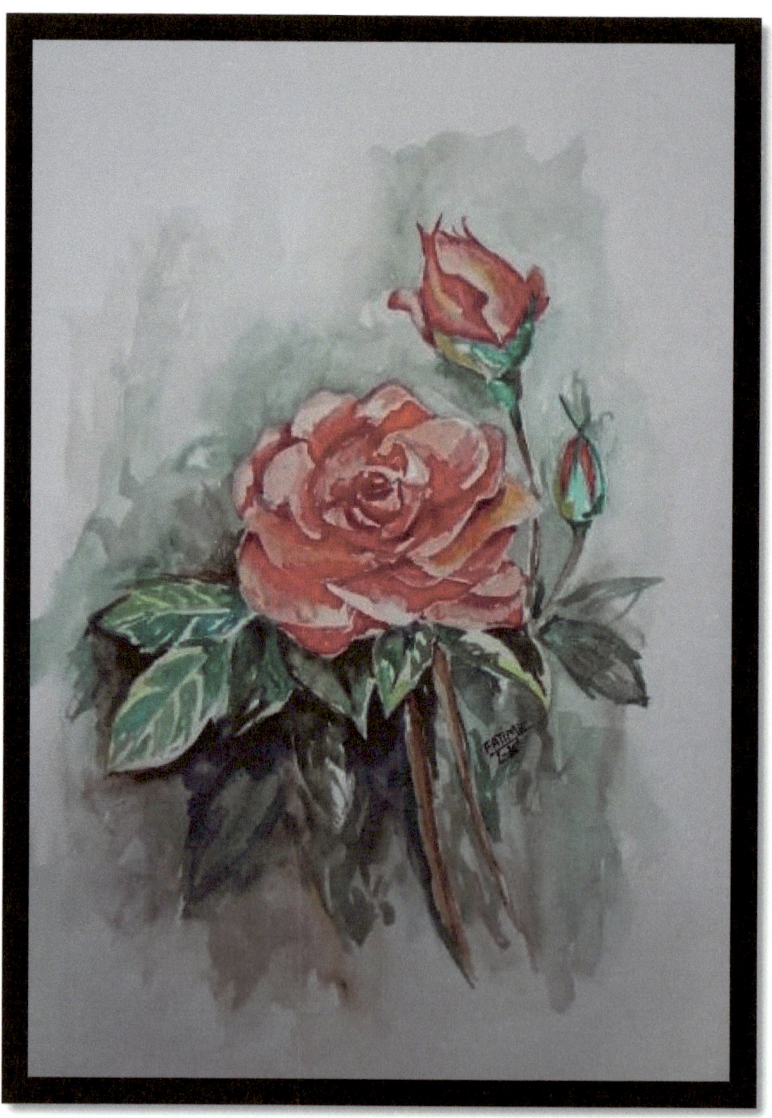

Image8.8

How to paint Tulips

Trace or draw some Tulips. I am making three Tulips, two in the foreground and one in background.

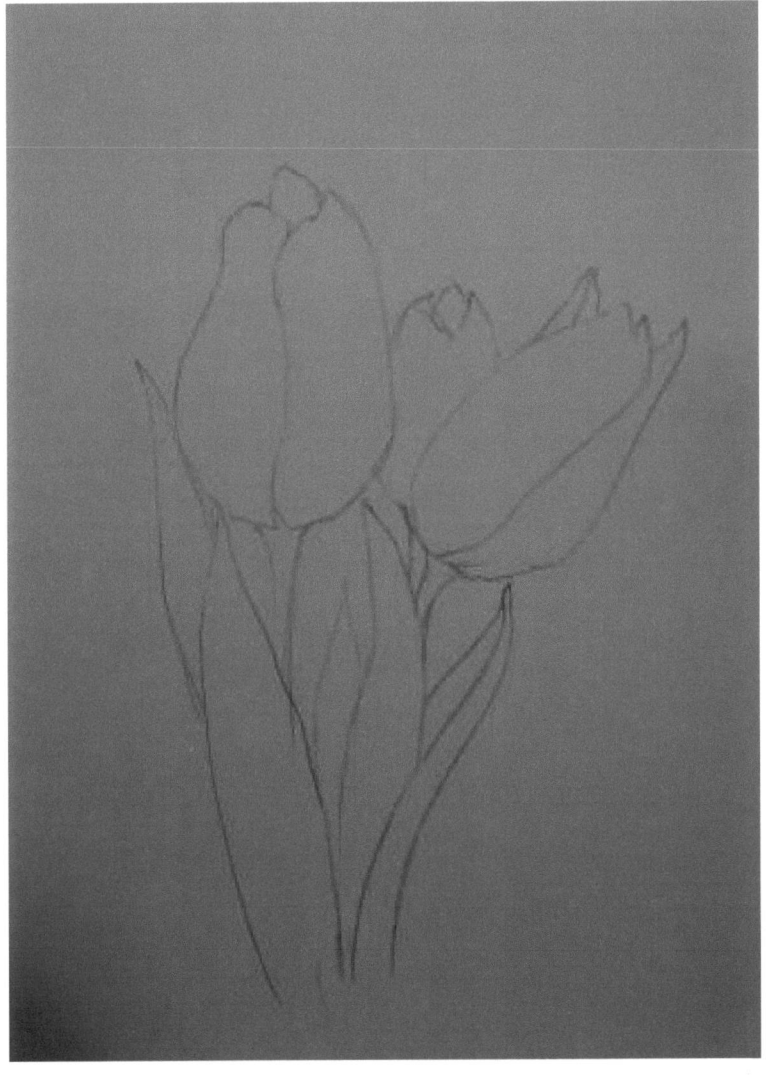

Image9.1

For the background, make it wet with a 1 inch brush and render it using No8 brush. Use considerably diluted red and Cad yellow. See your picture and paint the Darks in the flower first using Cad yellow. Do not dilute your paint a lot.

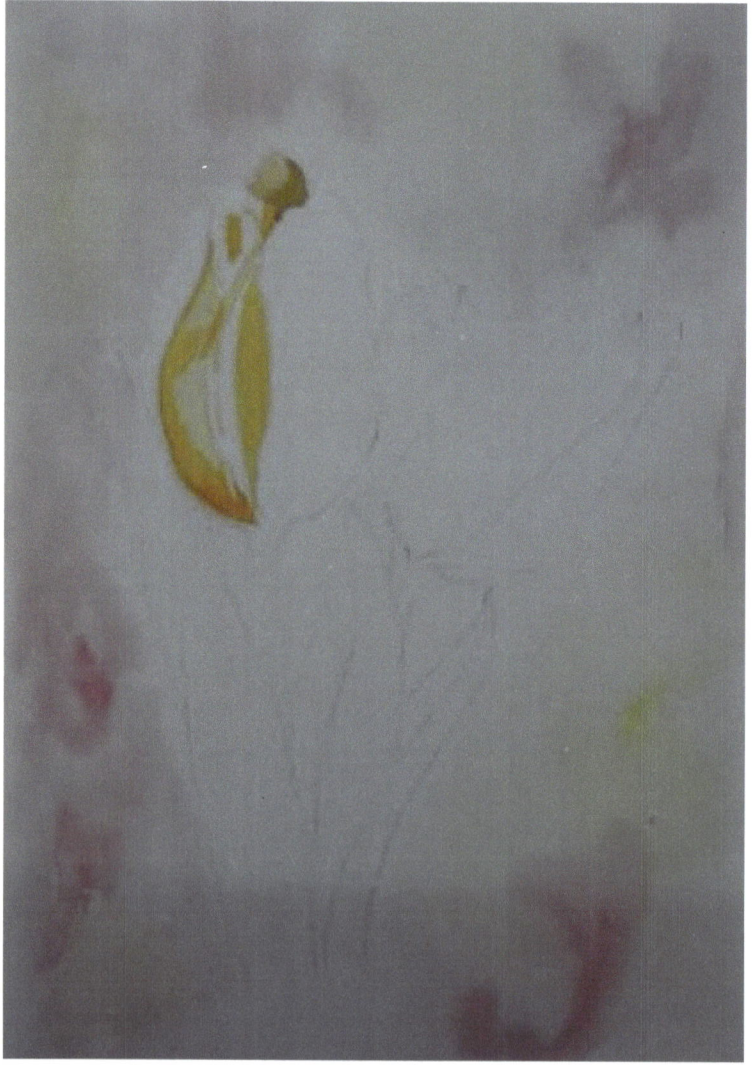

Image9.2

Use Yellow Ocher to paint the darkest areas. Start putting the middle tones. For the flower in the background, paint it yellow with much diluted paint. (See image 9.3).

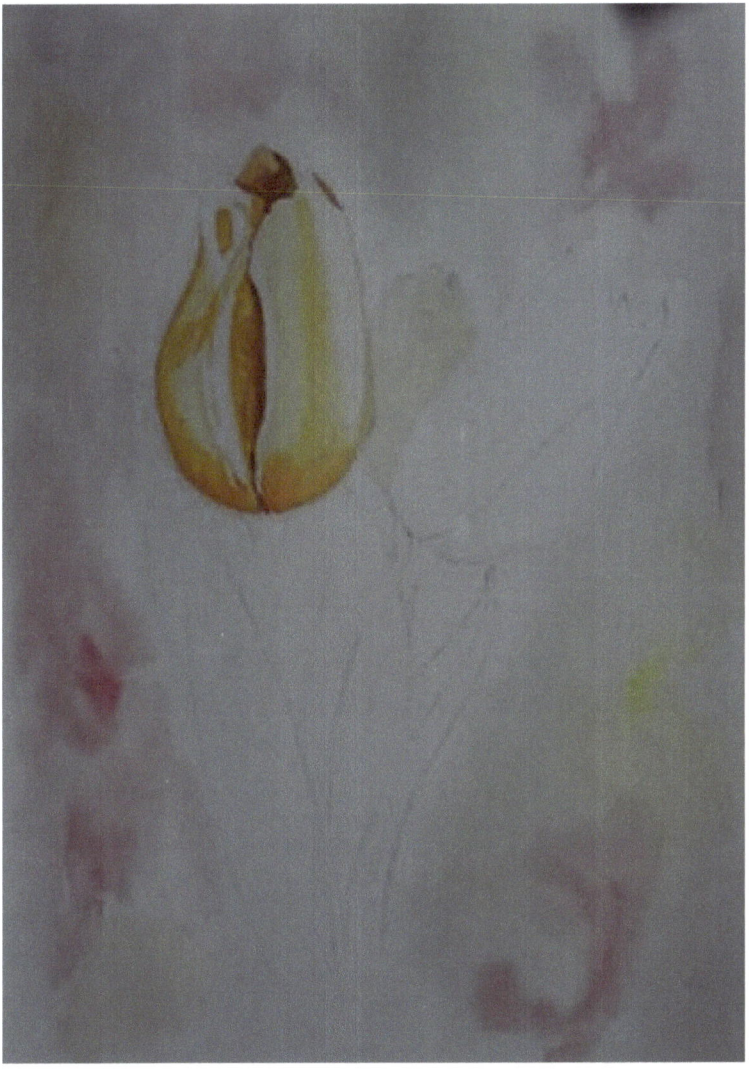

Image 9.3

Finish painting the middle tones and then add some green on the top edges of the flower. This will help your flower pop up. You can see that I have completed the flower by adding middle tones and merging them. (Image 9.4)

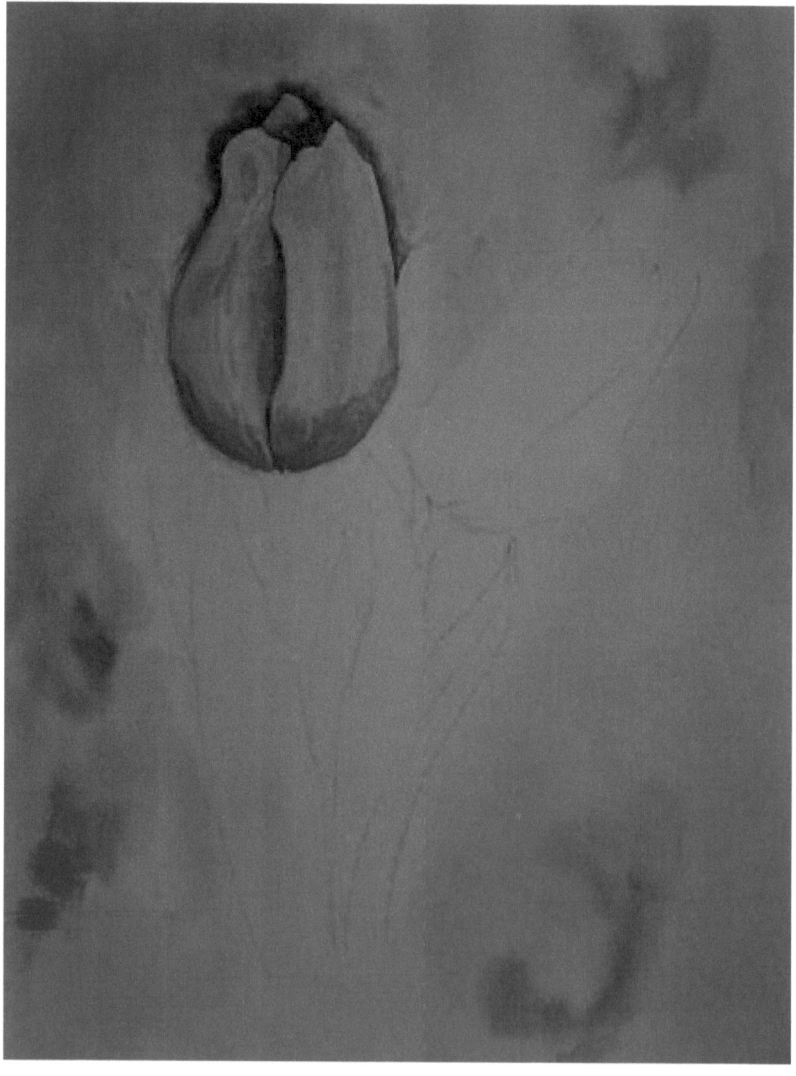

Image9.4

Paint the other tulip in the same way, use yellow to spot your darkest tones. Then to make them look darker, use yellow ocher. Paint the tulip at the back in the same way. (Image 9.5)

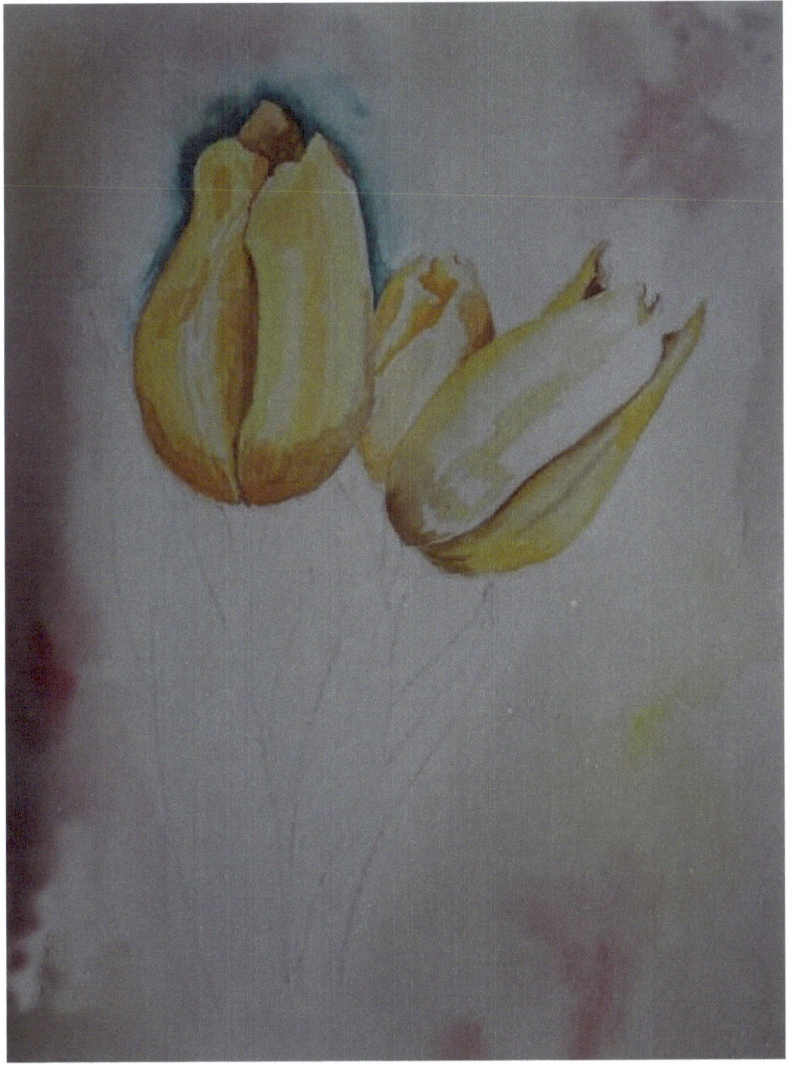

Image 9.5

Complete your tulip by adding the middle tones and adding green in the background. For the stem and leaves, use Hooker's green in very less diluted form to paint the dark areas. See Image 9.6

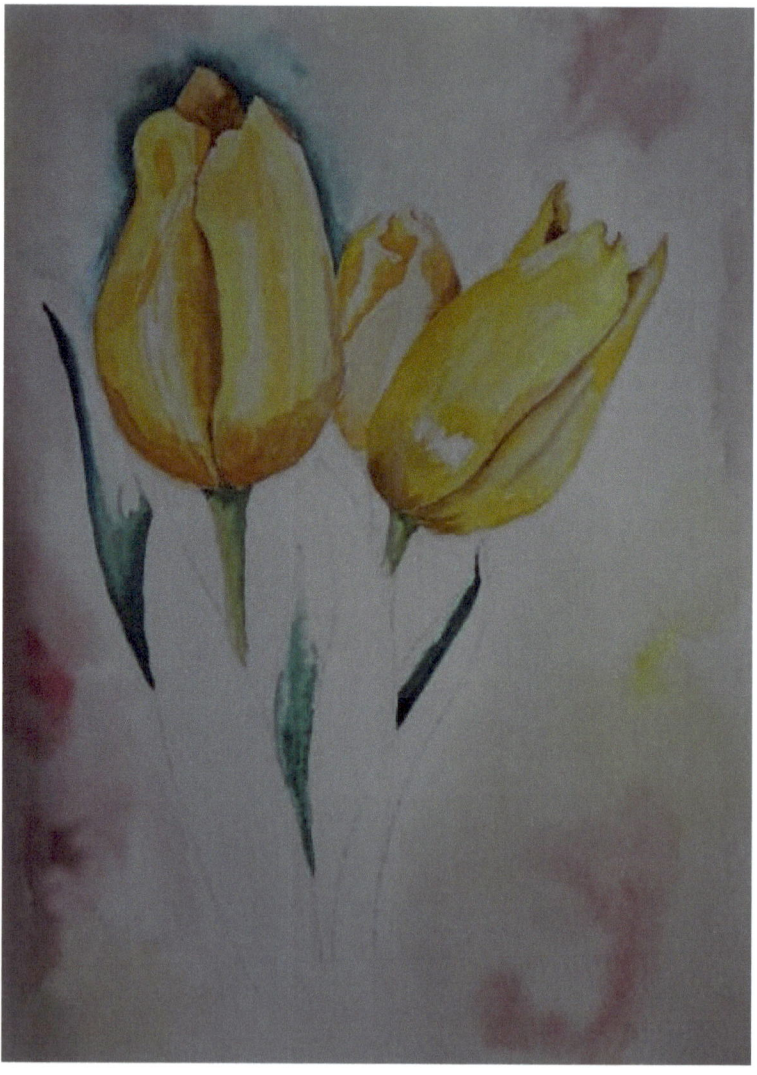

Image 9.6

Use Sap green to give lighter shades to the leaves. Blend the two shades of green.

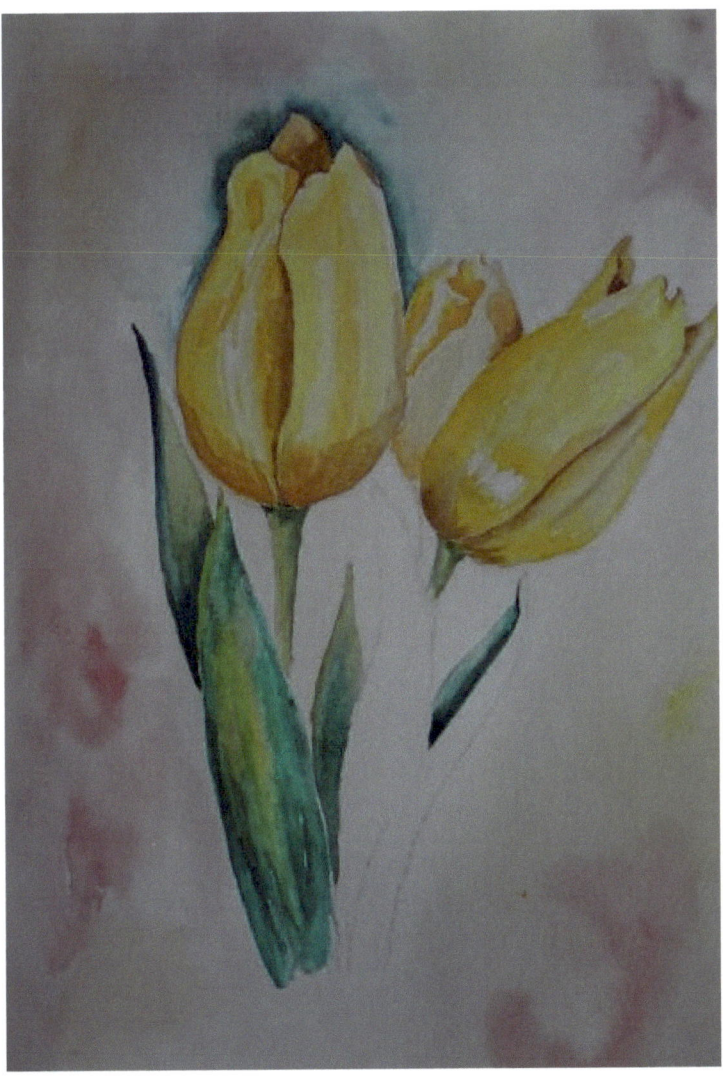

Image 9.7

Paint all the leaves in the same way. Start by adding darks and then use sap green for lighter tones (Image 9.8). Your painting is complete. You can now sign your painting.

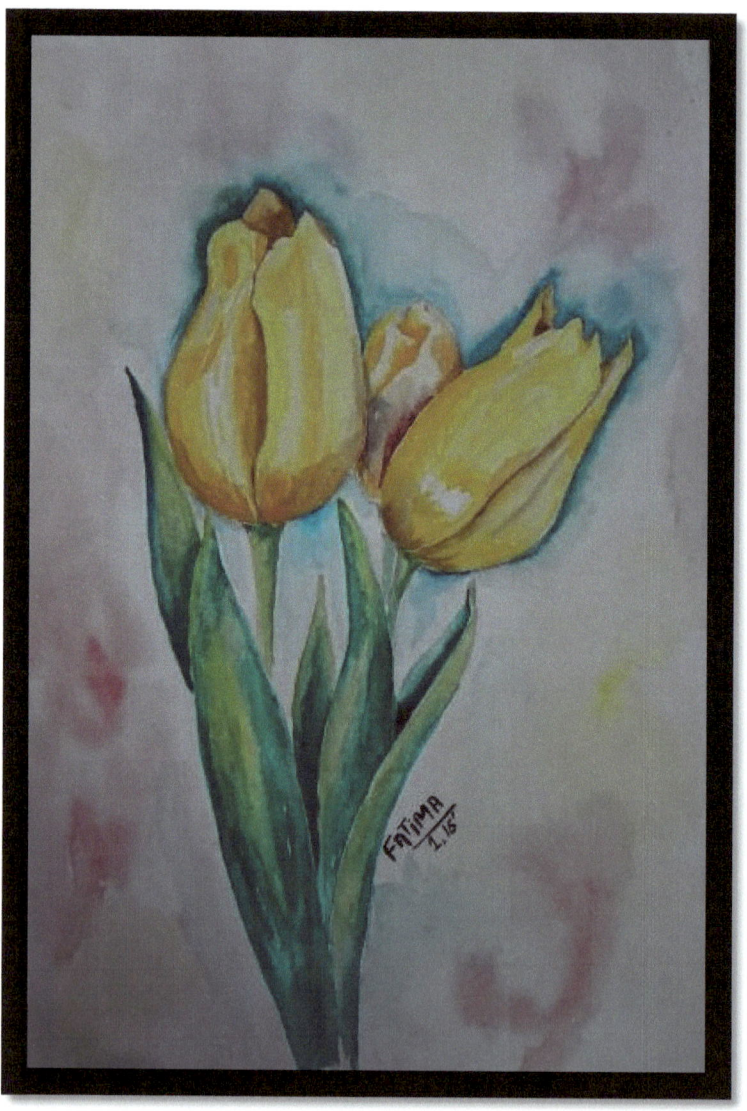

Image 9.8

How to paint an Iris

Trace an outline of iris onto your sheet.

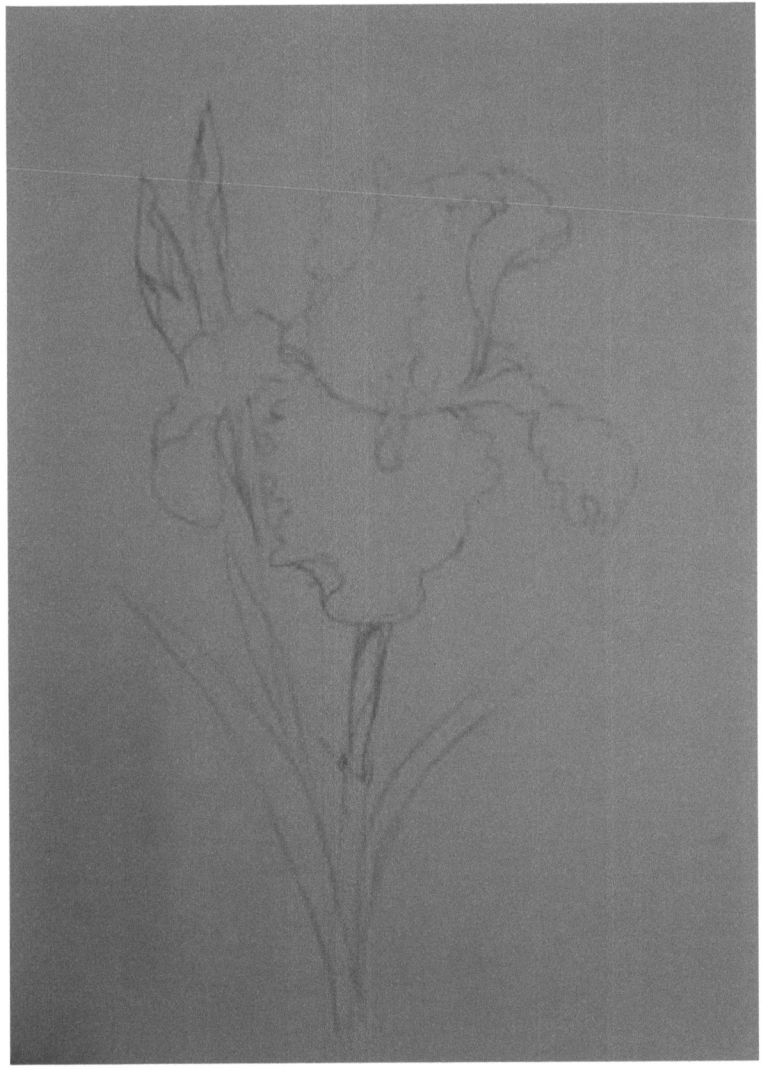

Image 10.1

Erase the lines but make sure you leave them visible enough for you to follow the shape of the flower. Paint the background as you have done in the previous paintings. Use burnt sienna for the background. Start with the leaves. Use dark green for the dark areas. I have used viridian tin for darks. You can use a color of your choice. Use sap green for light tones. See Image 10.2.

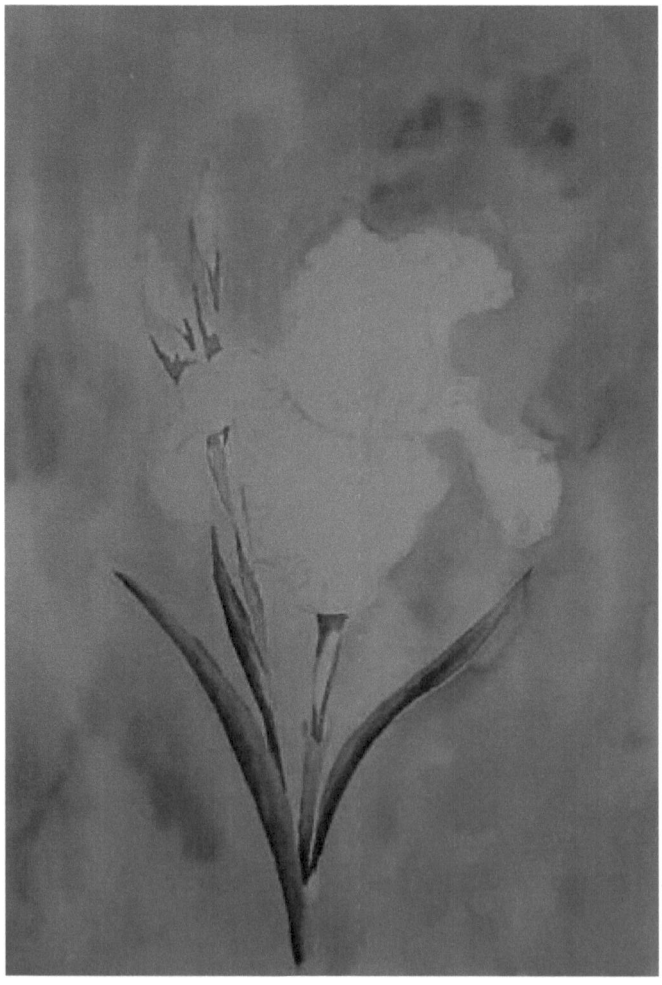

Image 10.2

Let's start with the flower. Take a purple color or prepare one by mixing red and blue. Do not dilute it a lot. Moisten the surface of petal that you are working on. Start by painting the dark areas of the flower see image 10.3.

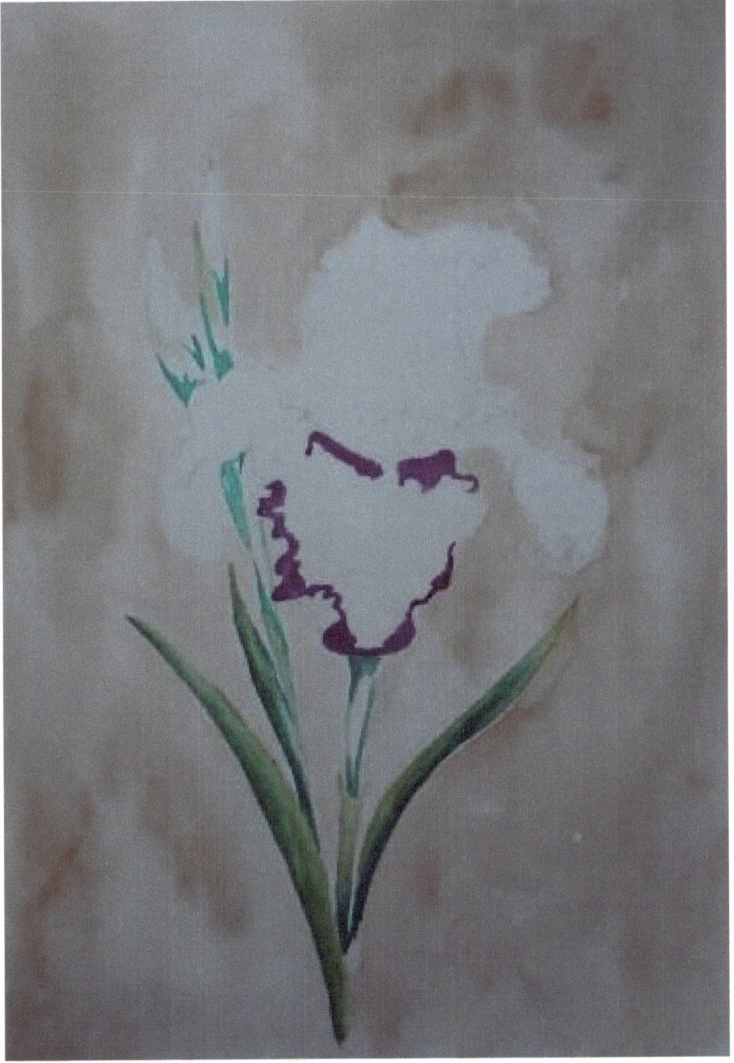

Image10.3

Next step is simple. Take much diluted purple and paint the rest of the area. Follow the lead of Image 10.4. Be very careful not to take too much paint. As purple is a dark shade, even the lightest tone may pop up pretty vibrant.

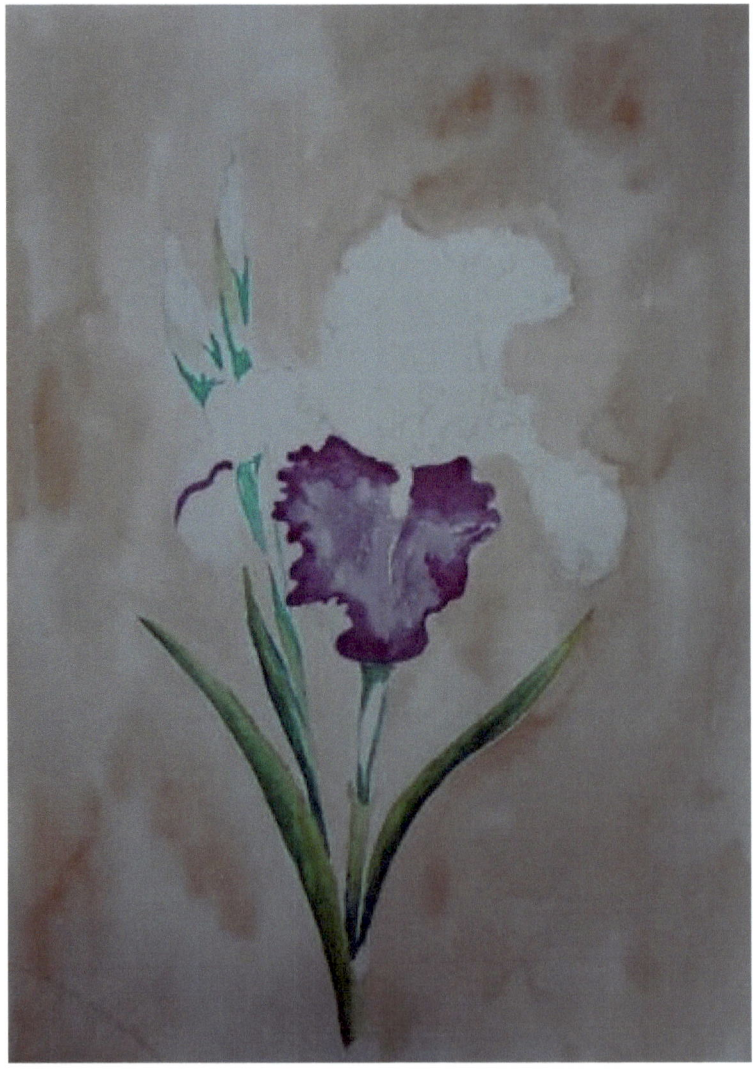

Image 10.4

Do the same with the Petals on the sides. Add the darks first then spread the paint with much diluted tone of purple to make the middle and lighter tones. See Image 10.5.

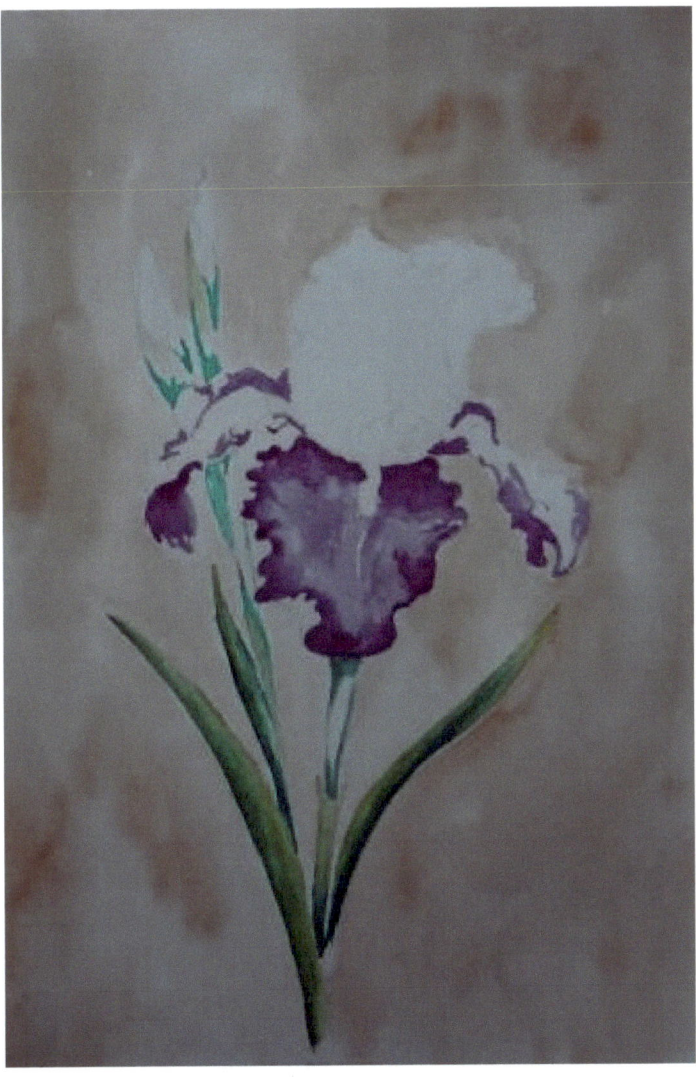

Image10.5

Now time to add life to your painting. Add Blue to the darkest areas. You can use Cobalt blue or ultramarine. Both will do well. Add orange to the centre of the flower and a bit of yellow as shown in Image 10.6. Add darks to the buds.

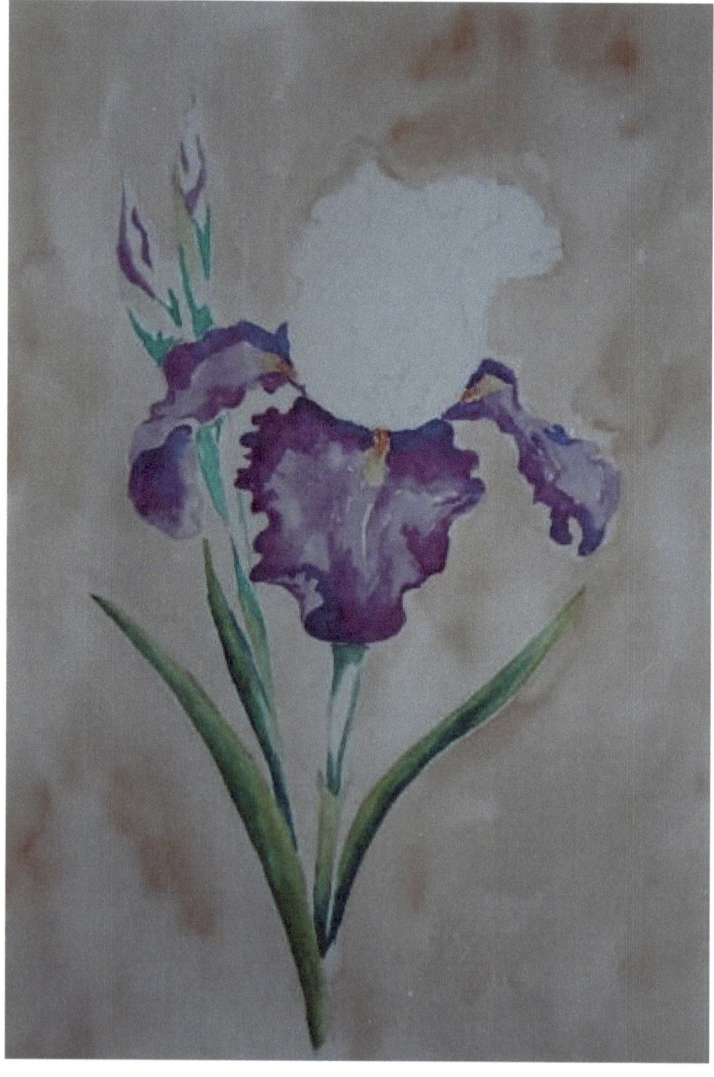

Image 10.6

For the white petals, use very diluted blue paint to draw fine outlines of white petals. Add medium tone to the buds to complete. Add a few more green leaves to give a lively look.

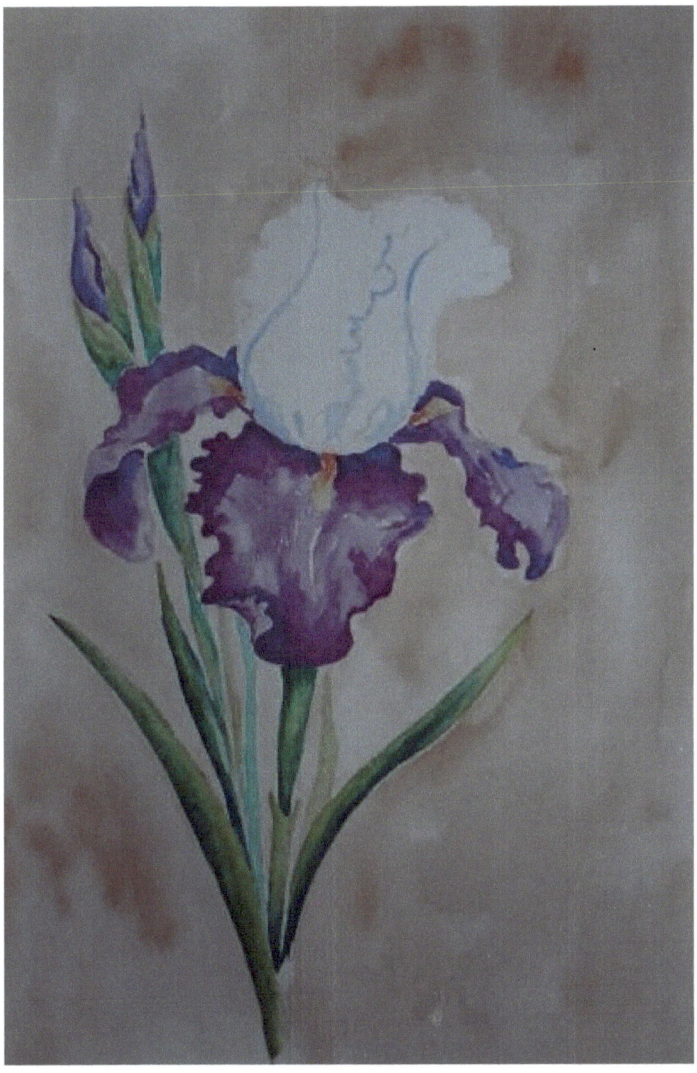

Image 10.7

Give shades to White petals with the help of blue. Remember to use much diluted paint. After you have finished, sign the painting.

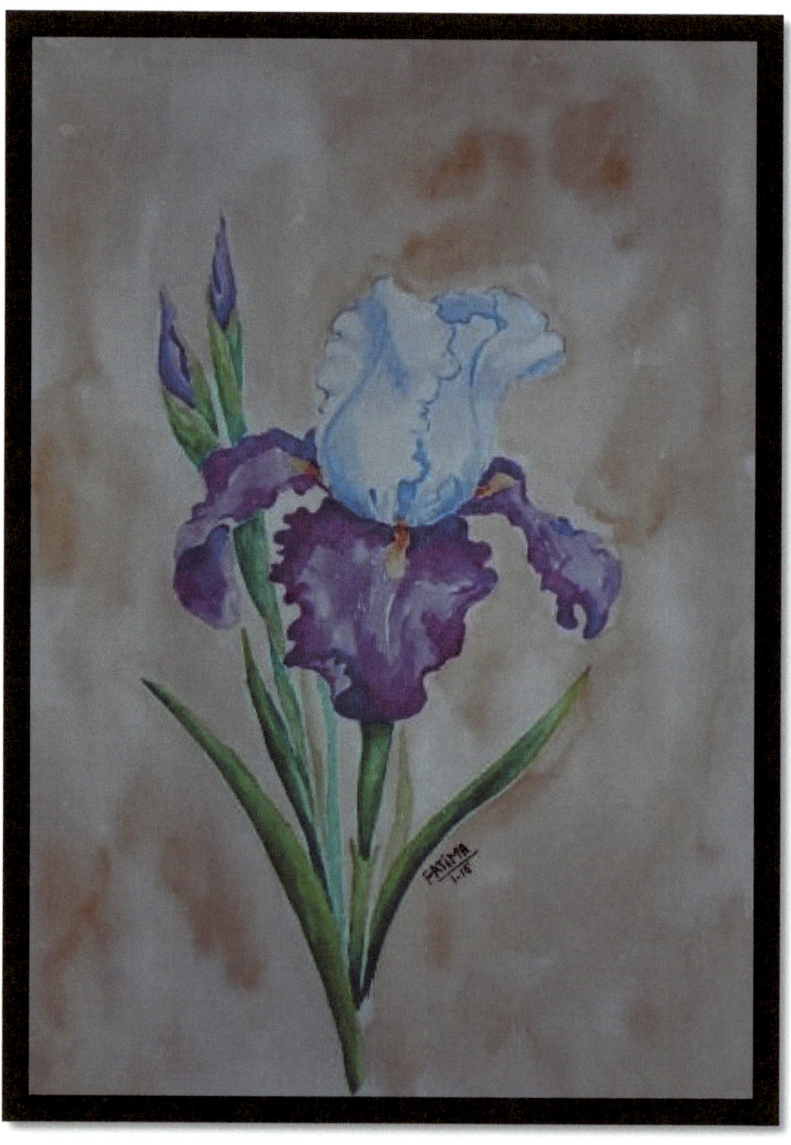

Image 10.8

How to paint a Sunflower

Find a picture of a sunflower; try to find an easy one that has few petals. Once you have painted one with few flowers and got hold of the technique, you will easily be able to paint heavy sunflowers. Trace the flower with a help of a tracing paper and transfer it onto your sheet (Image 11.1)

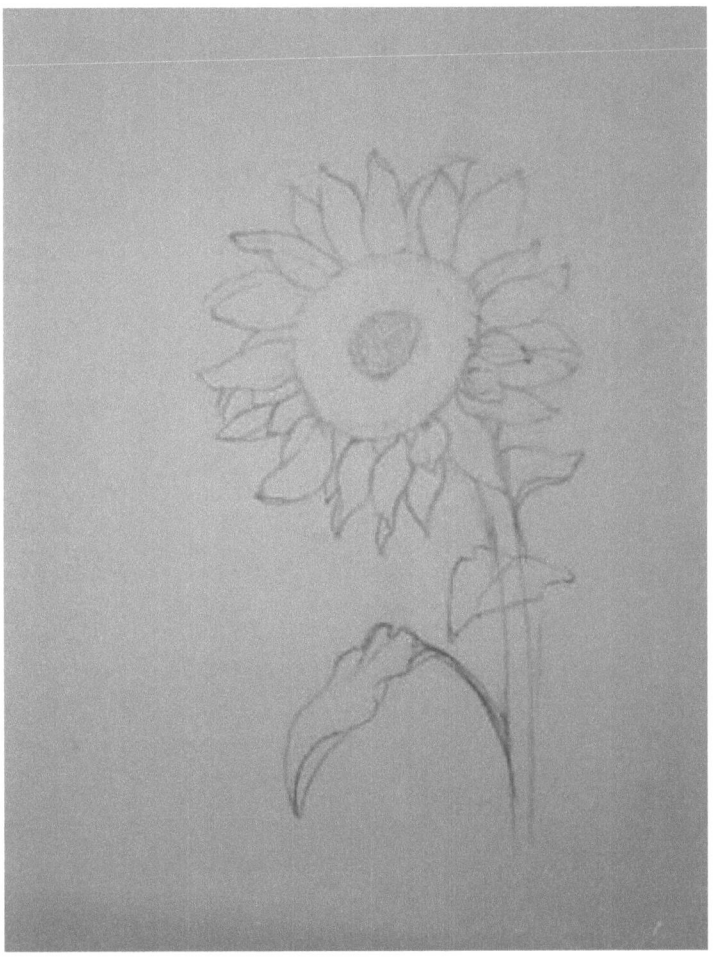

Image 11.1

Wet the background with your No8 paintbrush. Be sure that you only make the background wet and not the drawing. Paint the background (Image 11.2). Paint it in light tones of dark blue and burnt sienna. Take cadmium yellow and paint the petals in light tone. This will give you a base to work on. Paint the centre with burnt sienna and Hooker's green.

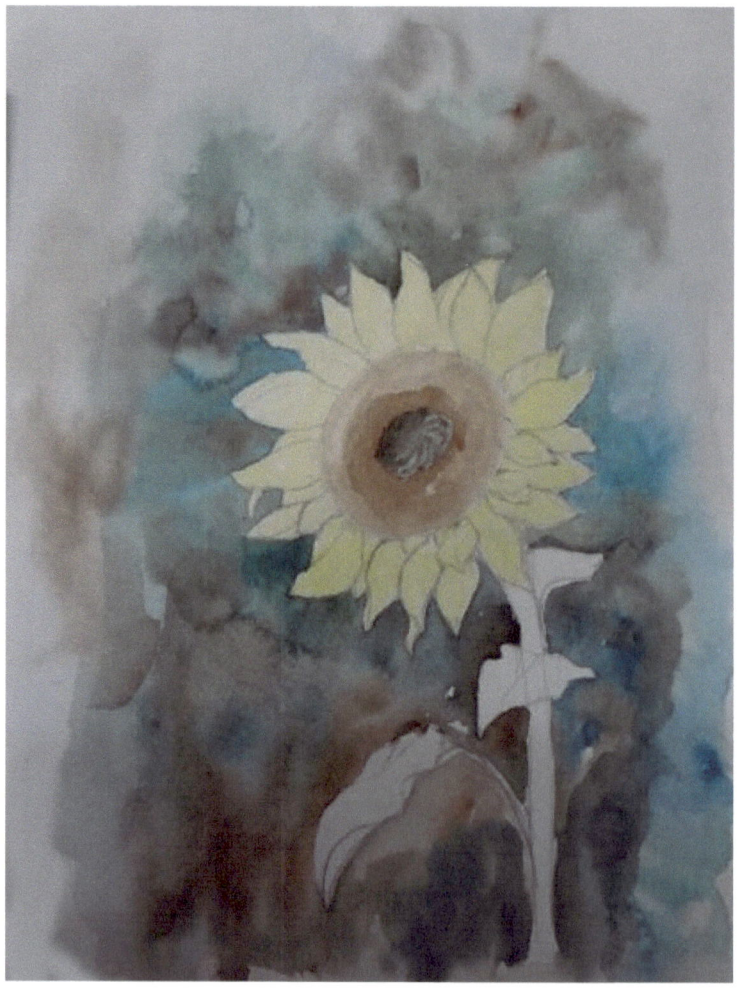

Image 11.2

Take cadmium yellow and orange tones to start painting the darker shades. In sunflower we will put the middle tone first and darkest tones last. Use sap green to paint the stem and leaves. (Image 11.3)

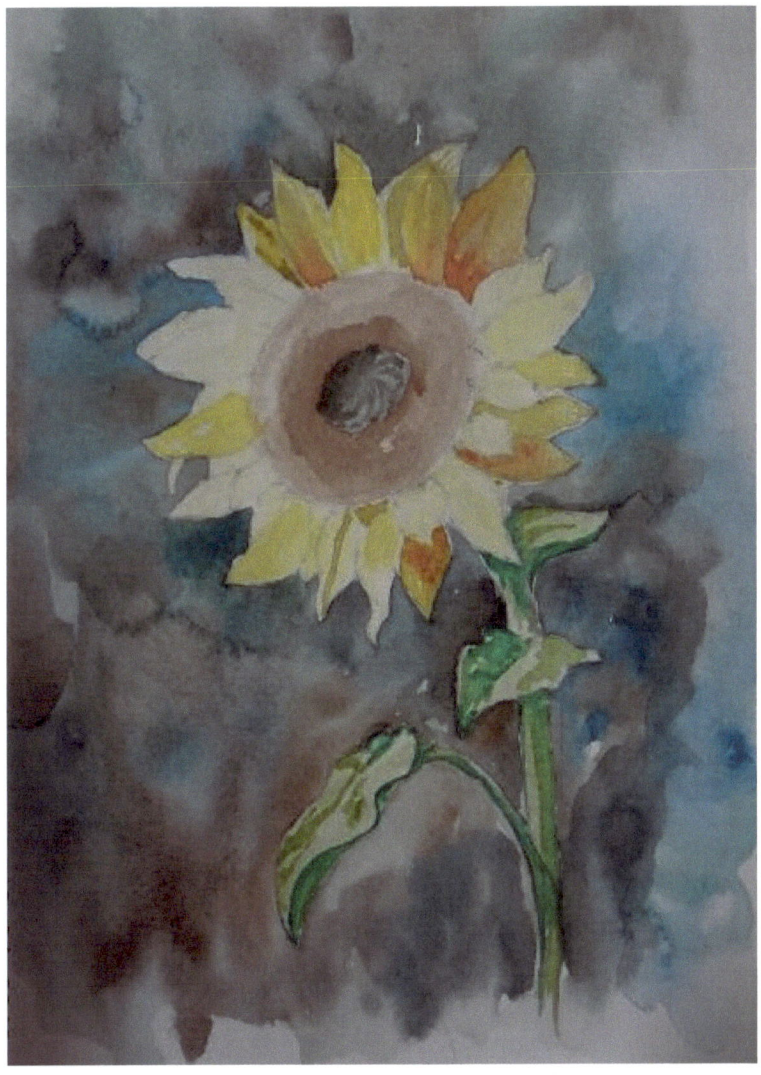

Image 11.3

In image 11.4 you can see that the flower is becoming alive. I have used Burnt Sienna for the darkest parts and insides of petals.

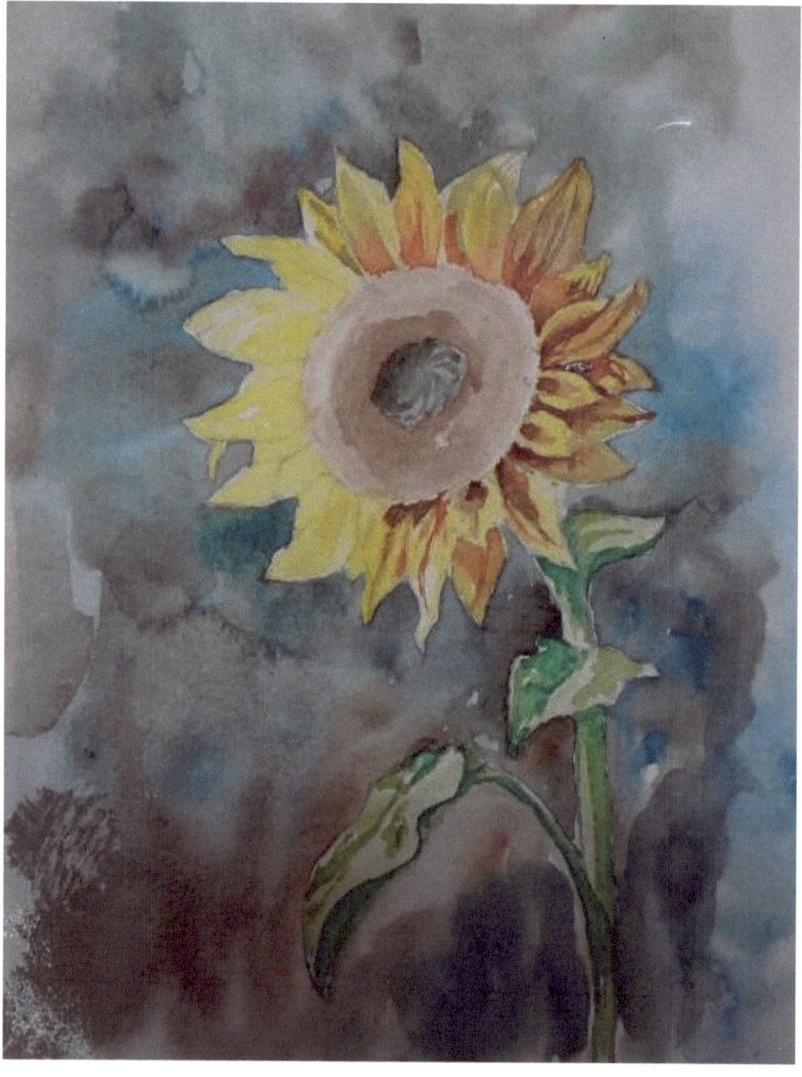

Image 11.4

Paint all the petals. Make sure you keep taking the reference from the picture because each petal is unique and it will need individual rendering. (Image 11.5)

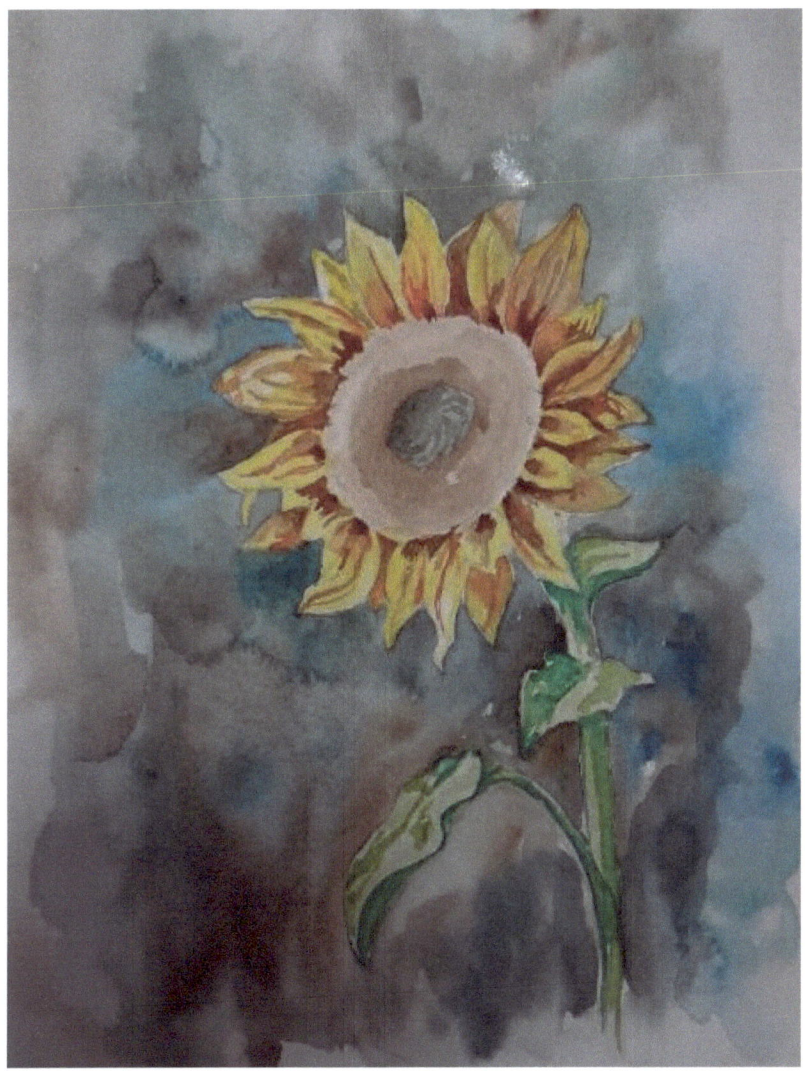

Image 11.5

We will now paint the core of the flower. Take out some lights and darks by using Yellow ocher for lighter part. Then take Burnt sienna and Raw Umber to put dots. Use raw umber for inner dots and burnt sienna for outer, for the centre use sap green.

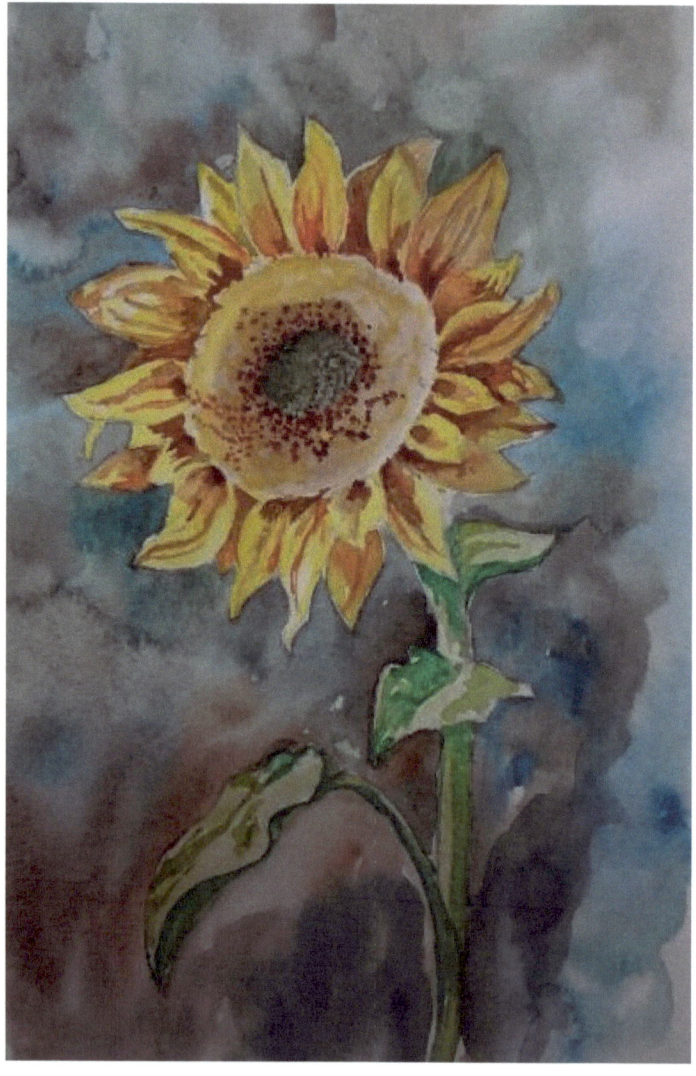

Image 11.6

You can see the complete flower in Image 11.7

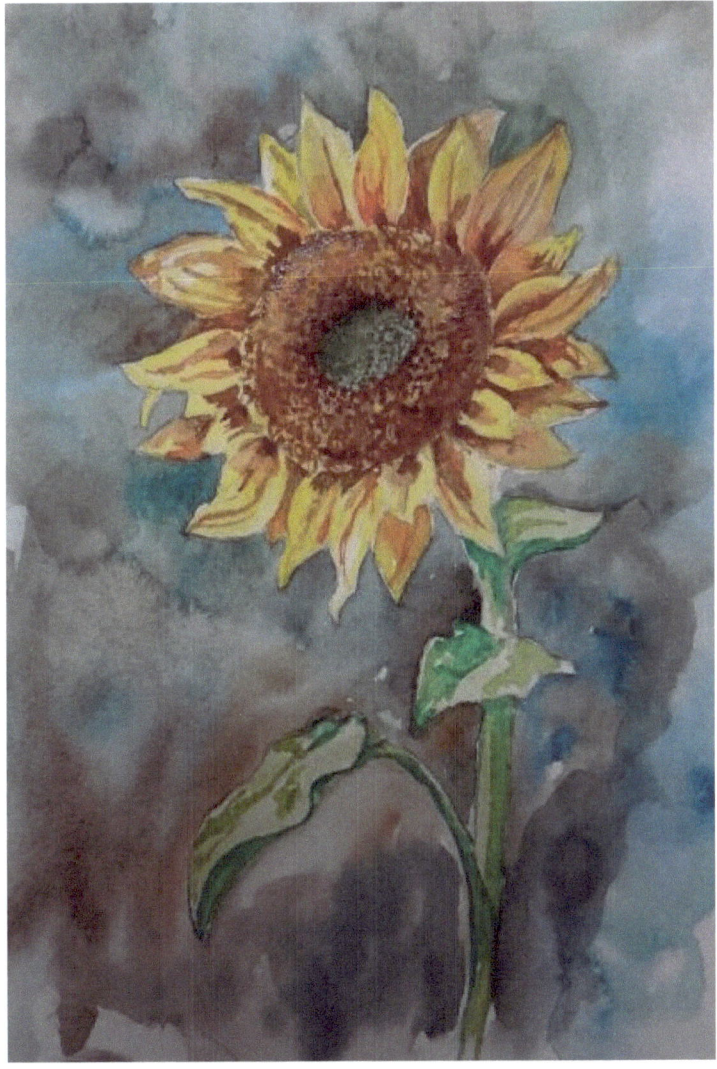

Image 11.7

Use some Payne's Grey to make the background. Make sure you dilute it properly; as very little color will have a great impact. Merge properly. The flower will stand out beautifully (Image8.8). Yep! Feed your pride, sign your name, claim your effort.

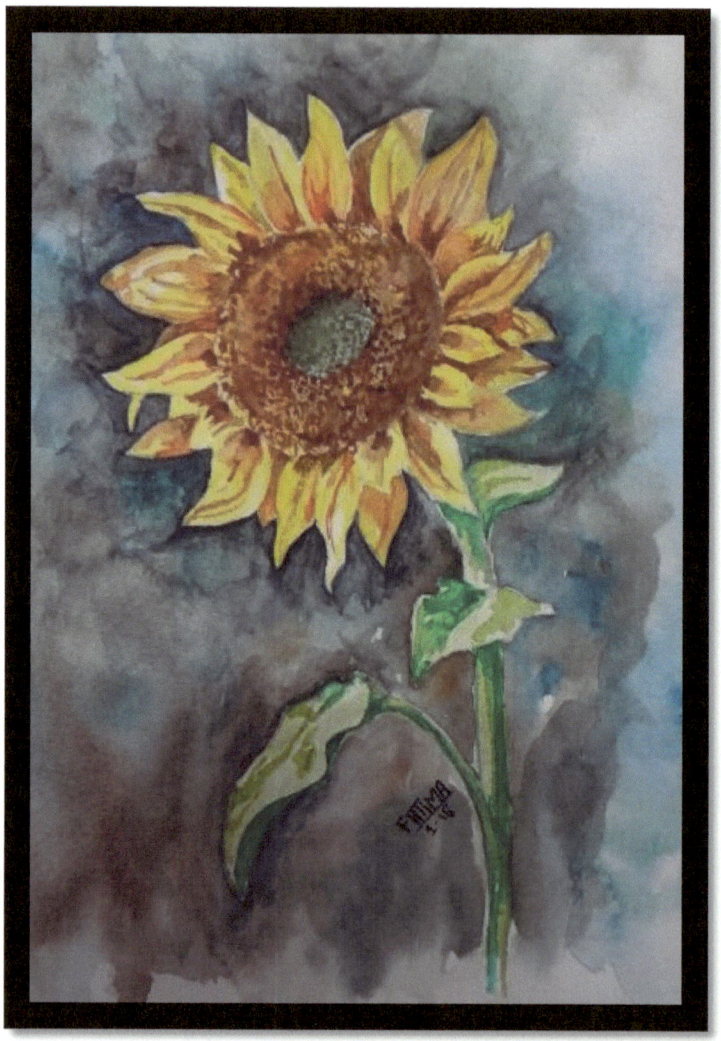

Image 11.8

Conclusion

If you work hard and strive for something, sooner or later you get it. So keep trying, you will get hold of this technique. It is not difficult, it only needs practice. Above all, don't think you can't do something. Nothing is impossible. You just need to practice a lot. Never be shy to ask questions or learn from the works of masters. If you see a painting, try to observe it carefully, you will learn a lot. Best of luck!

Artist Bio

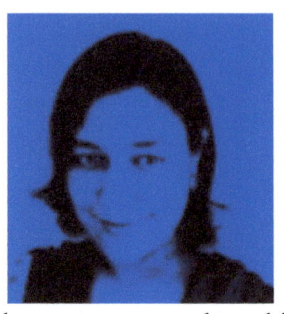 Fatima Usman has been awarded many certificates in the Field of Fine Arts. An expert in water color painting, she is also excellent with other mediums like acrylic, oil, pastels, sketching and many more. She is an observational learner, a hard worker and has got very good teaching skills.

You can reach out to her via email *FatimaMabbas@gmail.com*

Check out some of the other JD-Biz Publishing books

Gardening Series on Amazon

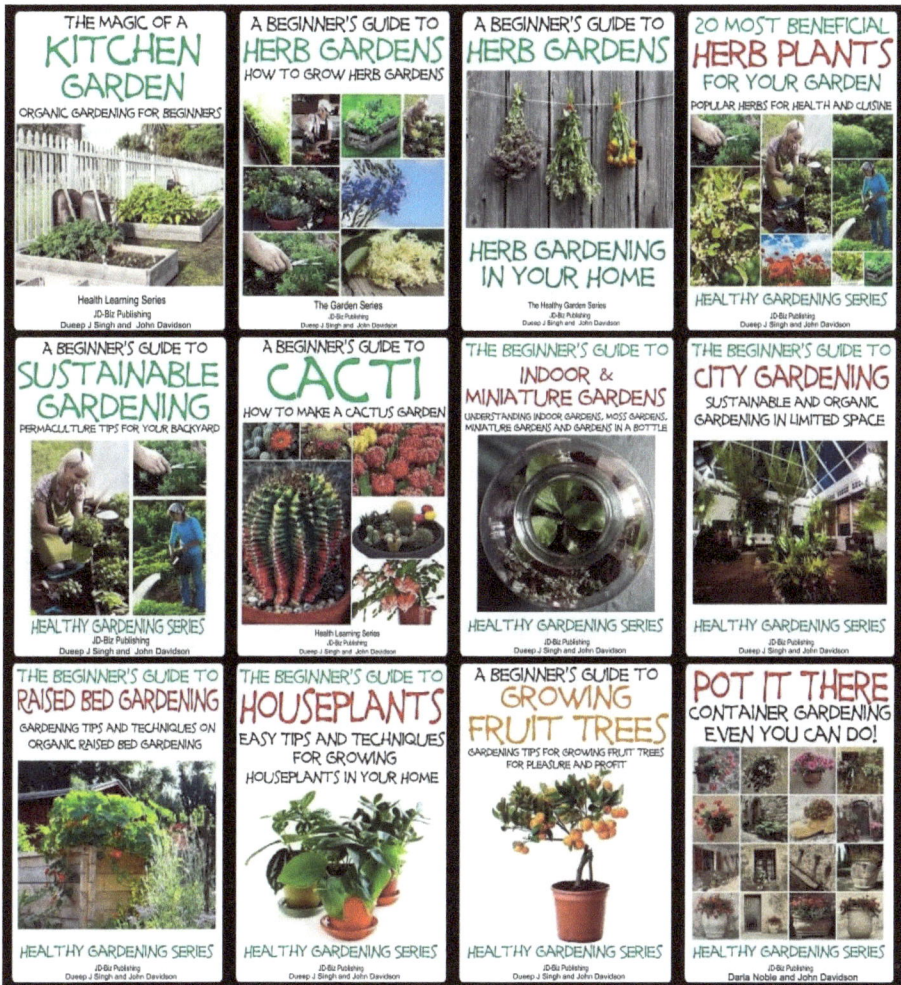

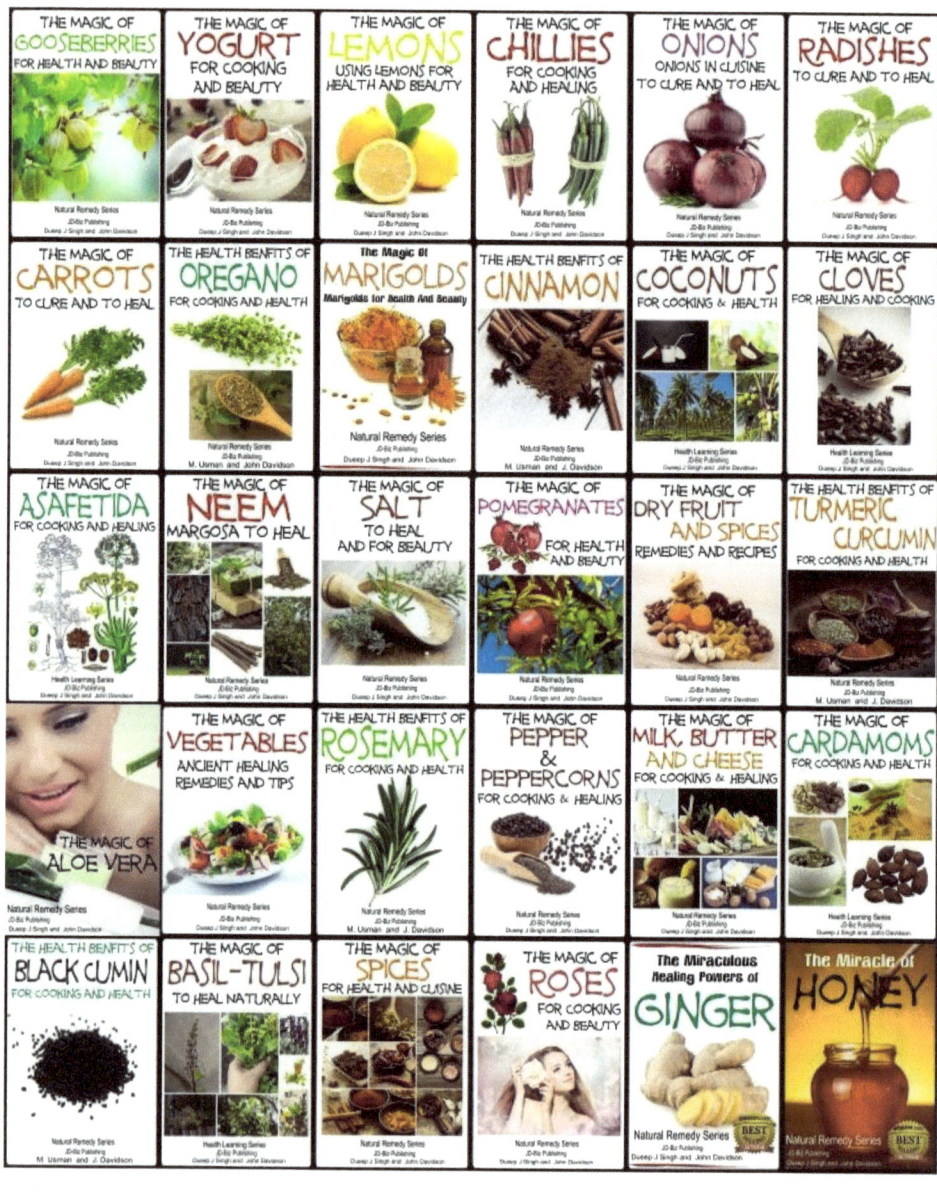

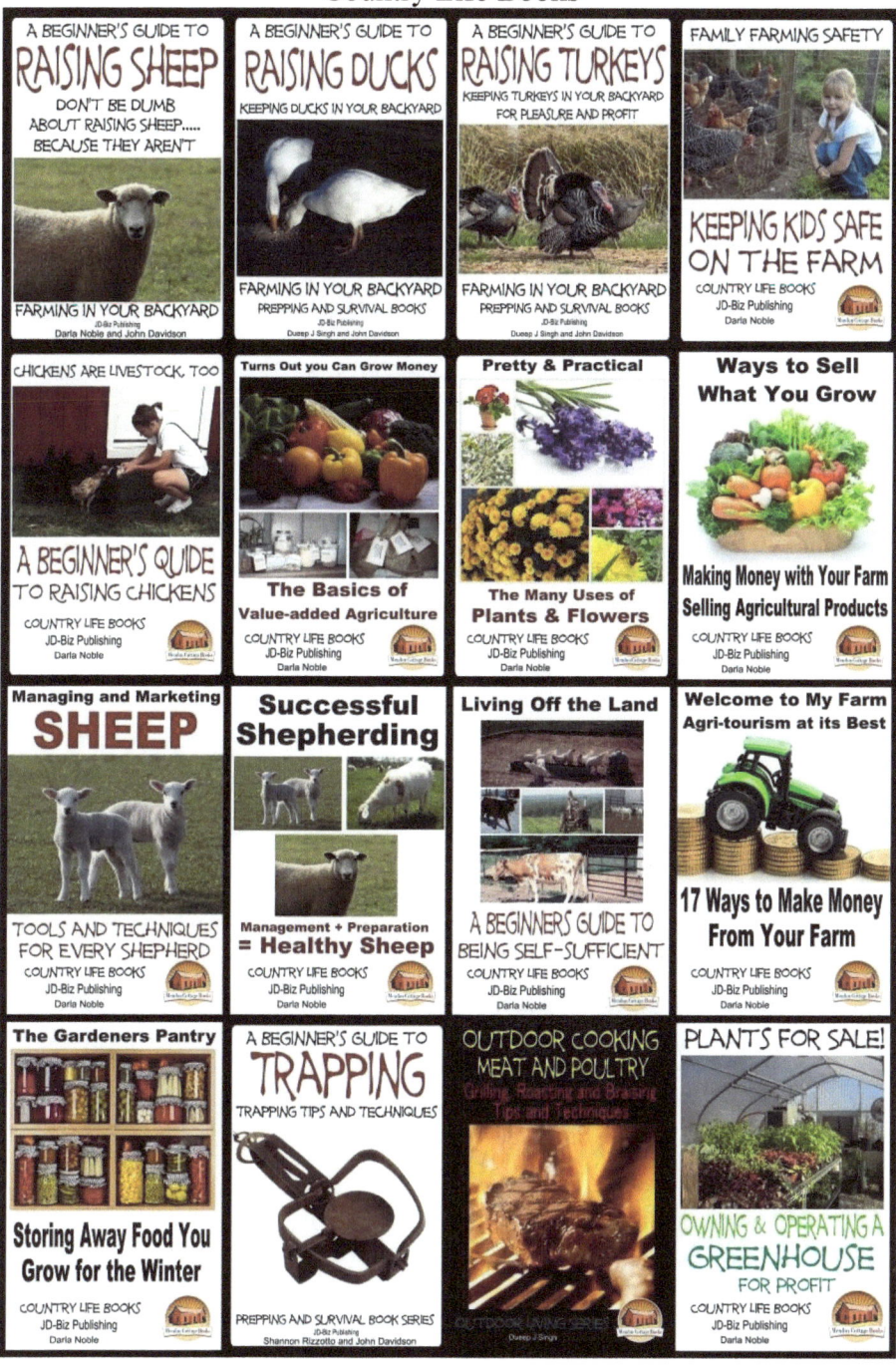

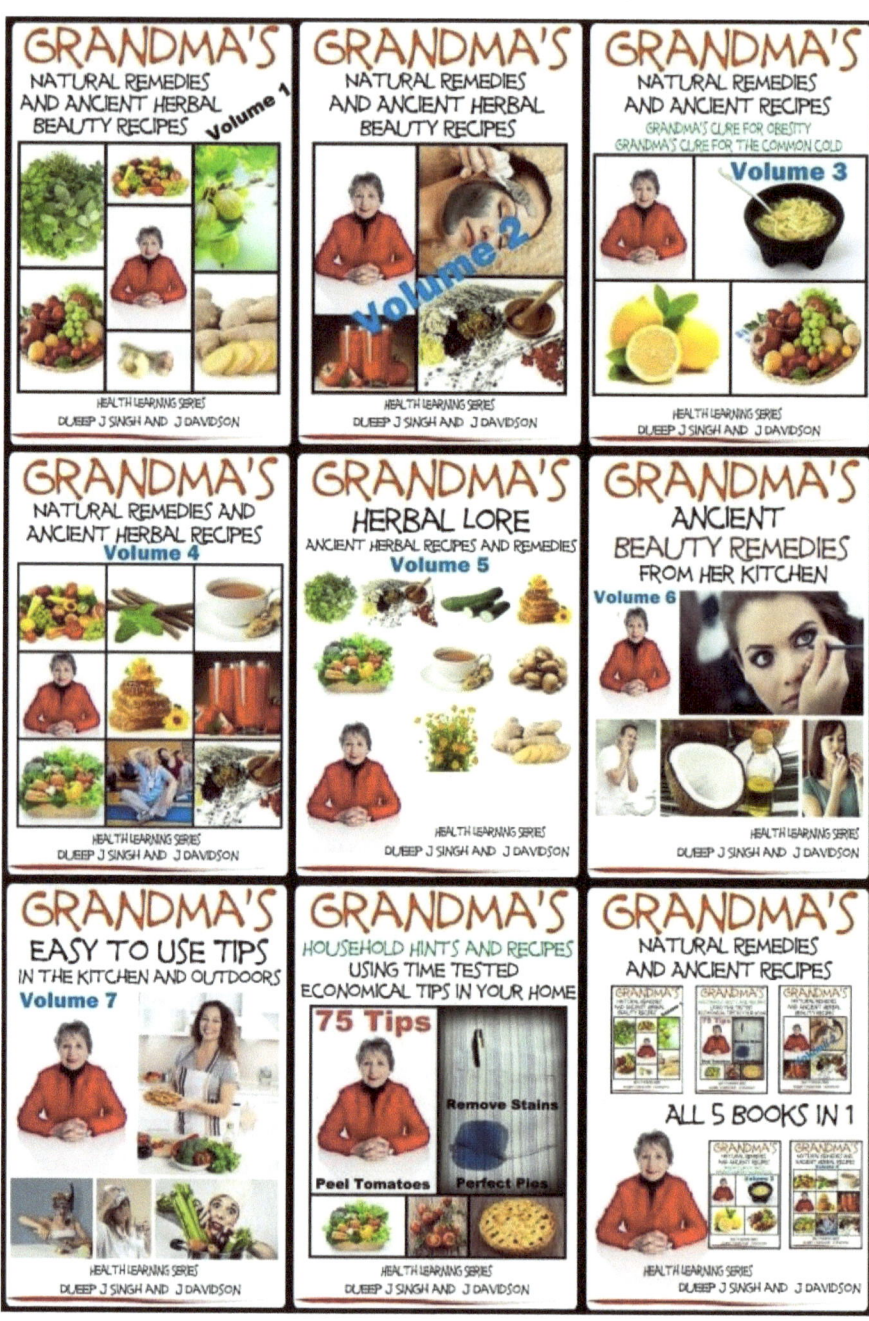

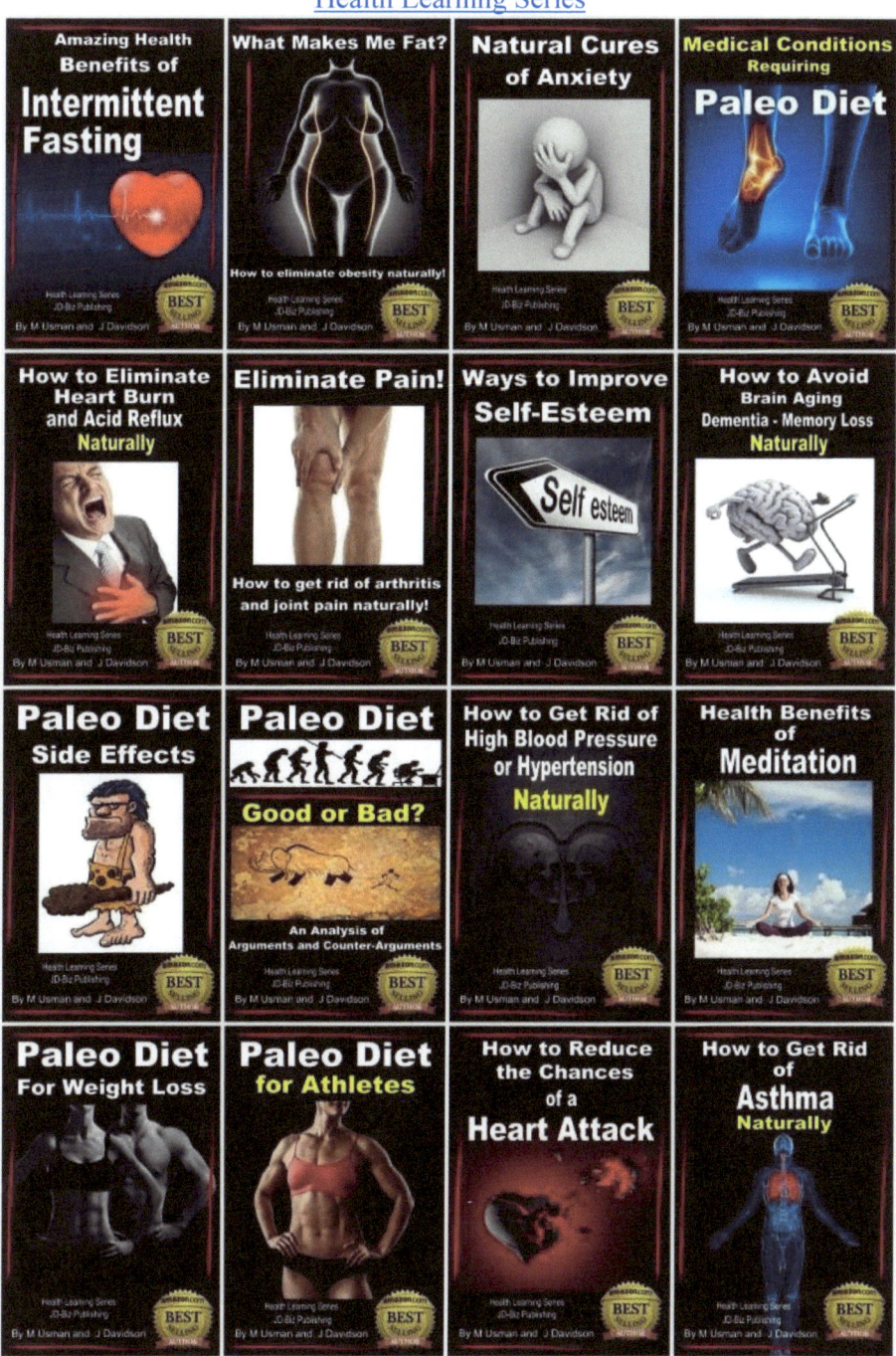

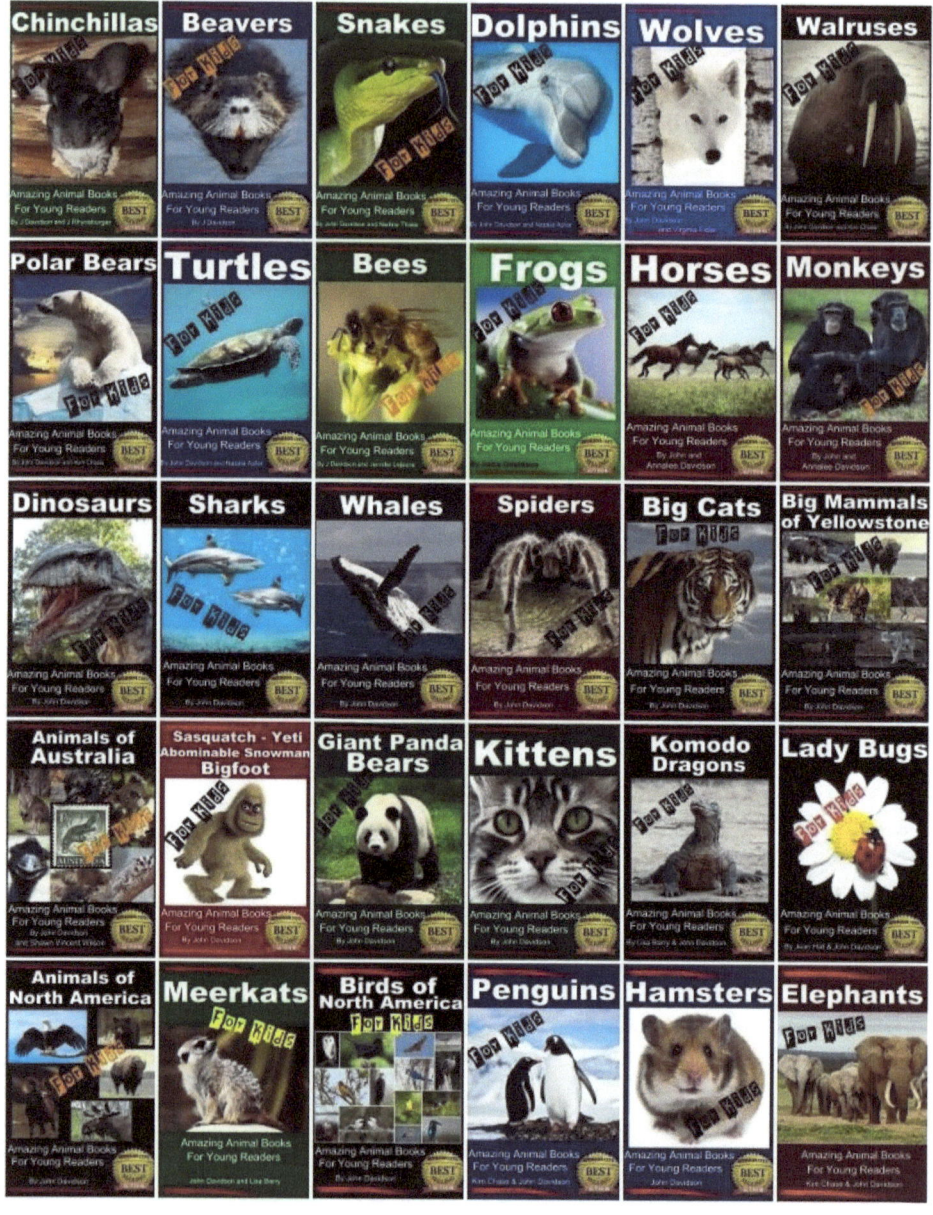

Learn To Draw Series

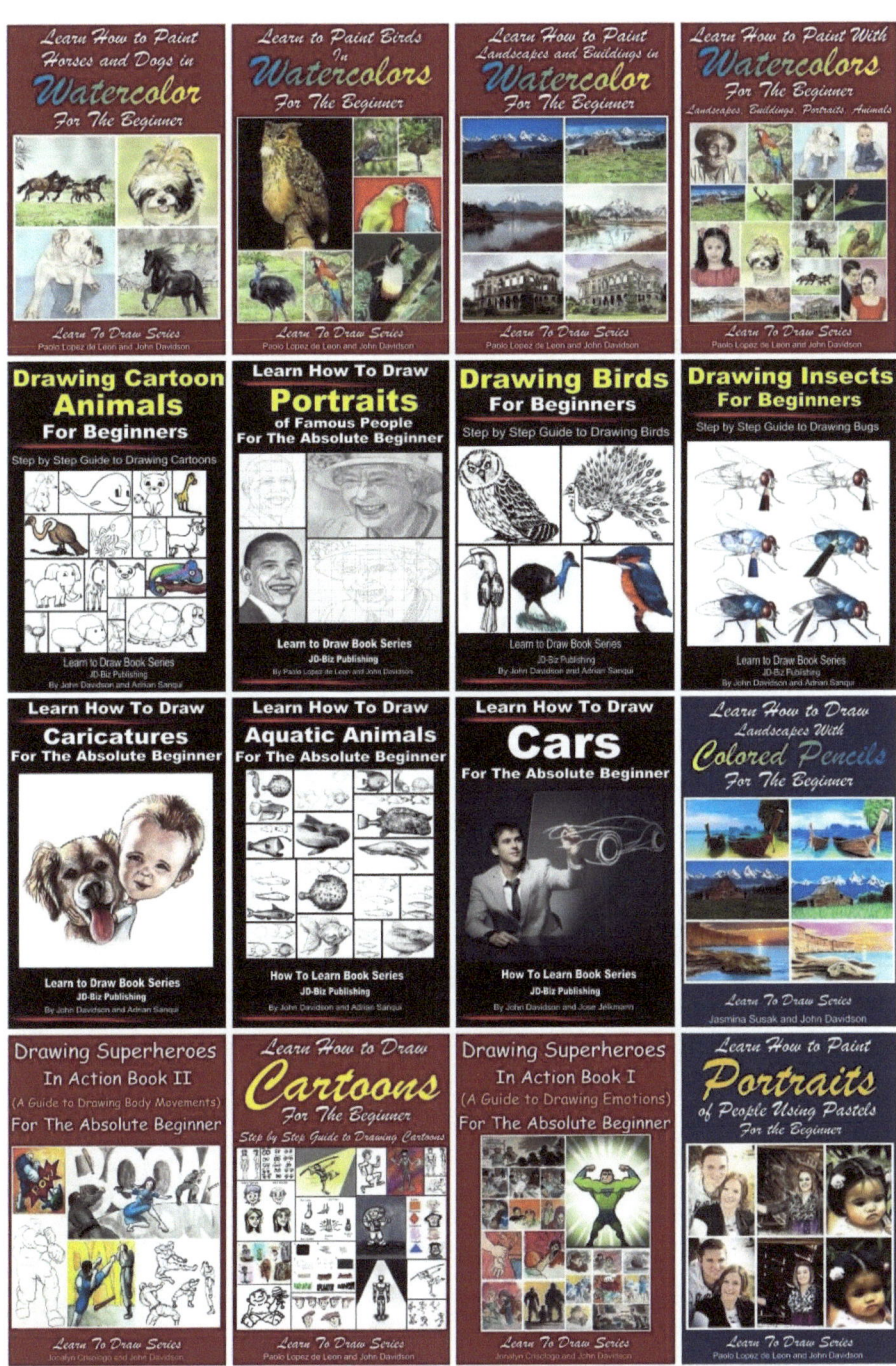

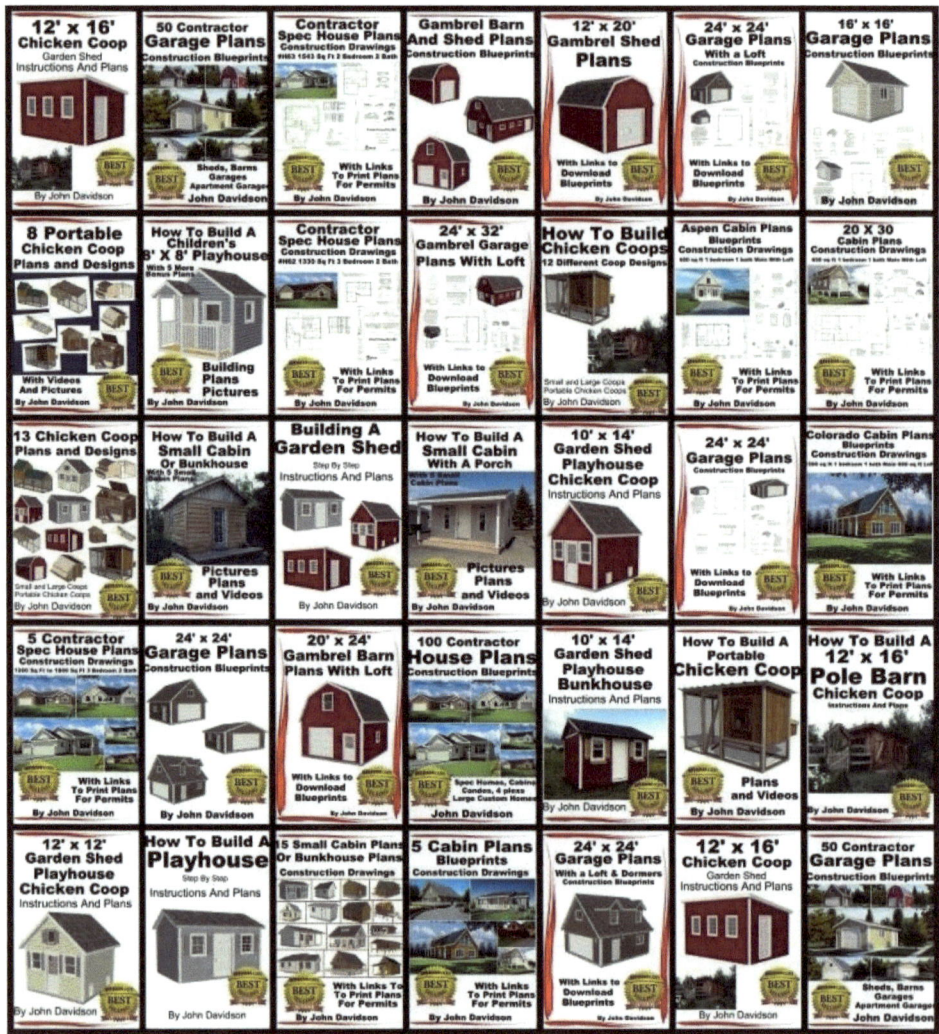

Entrepreneur Book Series

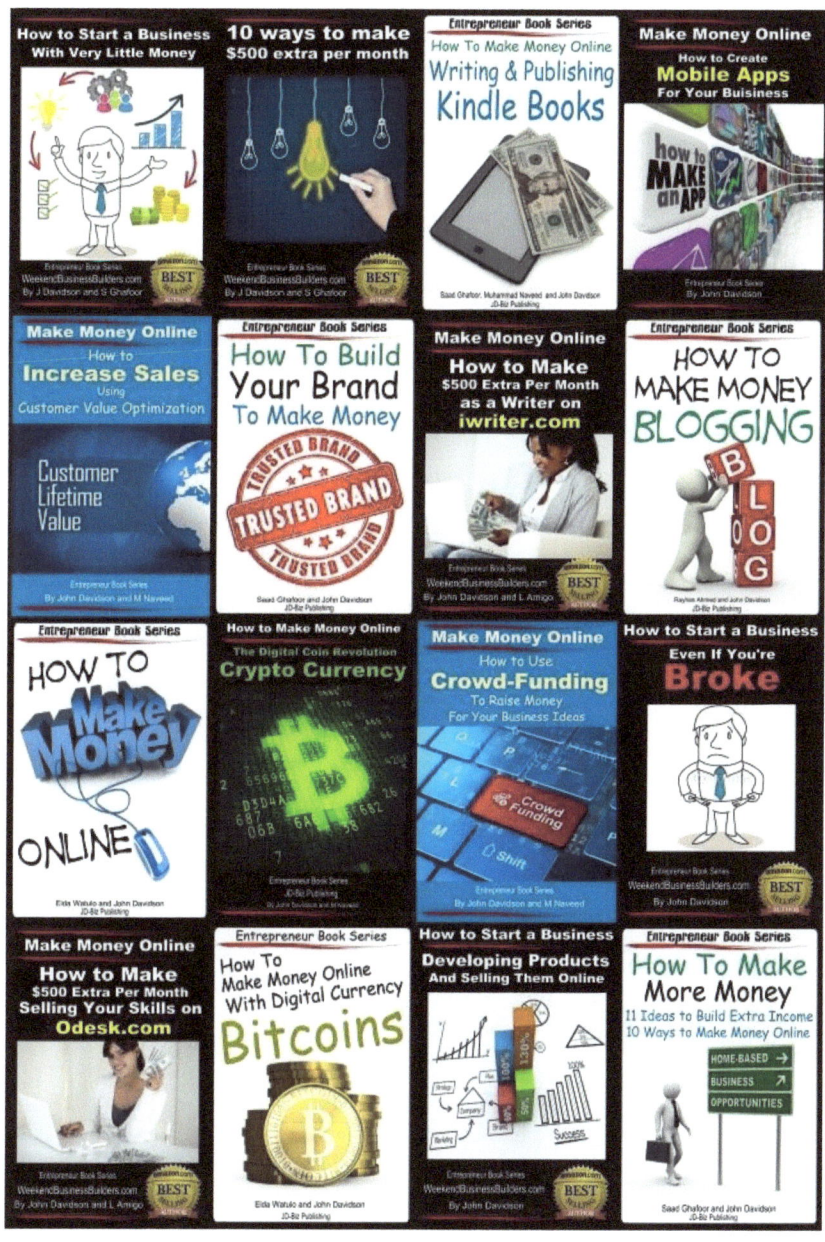

Our books are available at

1. Amazon.com

2. Barnes and Noble

3. Itunes

4. Kobo

5. Smashwords

6. Google Play Books

Download Free Books!

http://MendonCottageBooks.com

Publisher

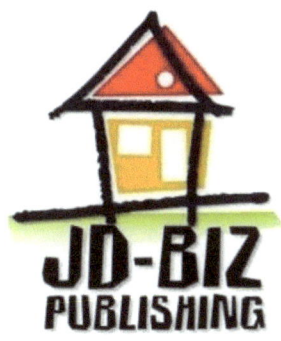

JD-Biz Corp

P O Box 374

Mendon, Utah 84325

http://www.jd-biz.com/

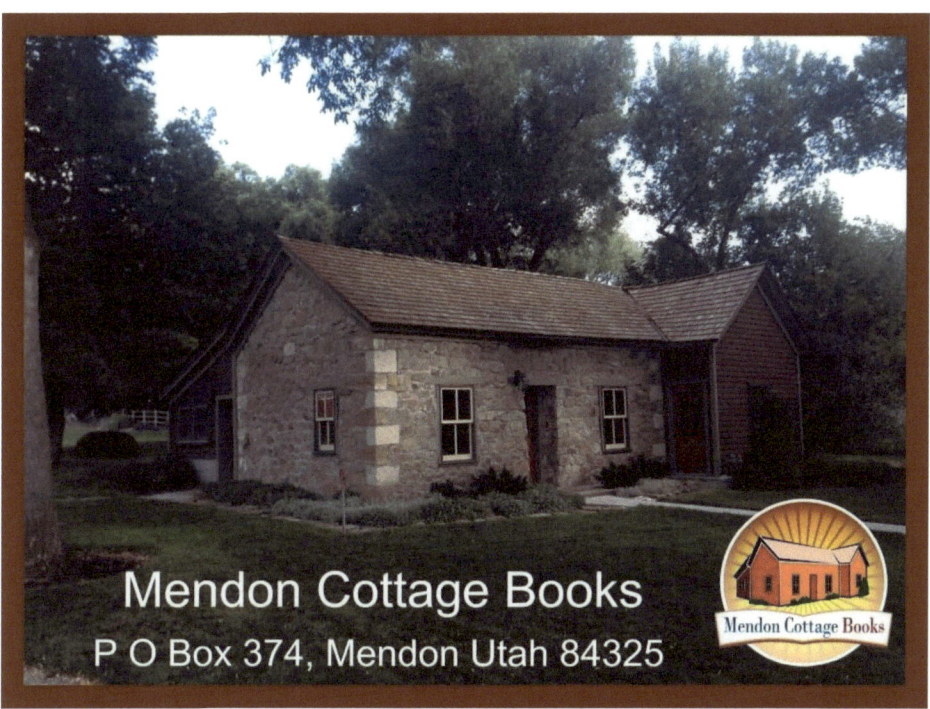

www.ingramcontent.com/pod-product-compliance
Lightning Source LLC
Chambersburg PA
CBHW040831180526
45159CB00001B/151